SO-BCP-529

Lights from the East

PRAY FOR US

J. Michael Thompson

FOREWORD BY
THE VERY REVEREND DR. PETER GALADZA

Liguori
LIGUORI, MISSOURI

Imprimi Potest:
Harry Grile, CSsR, Provincial
Denver Province, The Redemptorists

Published by Liguori Publications
Liguori, Missouri 63057

To order, call 800-325-9521
www.liguori.org

Copyright © 2013 J. Michael Thompson

All rights reserved. No part of this publication may be reproduced, stored in a retrieval system, or transmitted in any form or by any means—electronic, mechanical, photocopy, recording, or any other—except for brief quotations in printed reviews, without the prior written permission of Liguori Publications.

Library of Congress Cataloging-in-Publication Data

Thompson, J. Michael, 1953-
  Lights from the East : pray for us / by J. Michael Thompson.—First Edition.
    pages cm.
  pISBN: 978-0-7648-2337-4
  eISBN: 978-0-7648-6872-6
  1. Catholic Church—Oriental rites—Biography. 2. Christian saints—Biography.
  3. Catholic Church—Oriental rites—Prayers and devotions. 4. Christian life. I. Title.
  BX4710.9.T46 2013
  281'.520922—dc23
                        2013032015

Scripture texts in this work are taken from the *New American Bible*, revised edition © 2010, 1991, 1986, 1970 Confraternity of Christian Doctrine, Washington, D.C., and are used by permission of the copyright owner. All Rights Reserved. No part of the *New American Bible* may be reproduced in any form without permission in writing from the copyright owner.

Excerpts from Vatican documents © *Libreria Editrice Vaticana*.

The contents of the "Quotations" sections of this book are from the *Menaion*, a work that includes the hymn, prayers, and readings honoring each saint on the Byzantine calendar. The quotations are the author's translations of Byzantine texts. The sources are listed on page 144.

Hymns typeset by Jeff Mierzejewski

Liguori Publications, a nonprofit corporation, is an apostolate of The Redemptorists. To learn more about The Redemptorists, visit Redemptorists.com.

Printed in the United States of America
17 16 15 14 13 / 5 4 3 2 1
First Edition

CONTENTS

About the Author

J. Michael Thompson of Pittsburgh—known for choral and liturgical work as an author, editor, and composer—founded the *Schola Cantorum* of St. Peter the Apostle and is its artistic director. Thompson—who earned a master's degree in church music from Concordia University in River Forest, Illinois—also has served as professor of ecclesiastical chant at the Byzantine Catholic Seminary of Saints Cyril and Methodius in Pittsburgh and was the cantor/director of music at the Byzantine Catholic Cathedral of Saint John the Baptist in Munhall, Pennsylvania.

FOREWORD

The following words were written in 1935 by a bishop who no doubt will soon be included in publications similar to the present book by J. Michael Thompson. They are from the pen of Metropolitan Andrey Sheptytsky (1865–1944), the Ukrainian Greco-Catholic hierarch who sheltered hundreds of Jews during the Holocaust.

In the word "holy" lies a depth surpassing every conceivable thought. It is absolutely inaccessible—even to the greatest intellect. In that word there exists a grandeur, a transcendence, an incomprehensibility! "Holy" expresses the impossibility of attaining or grasping the Light that none can approach. In other words, it expresses the impossibility of comprehending or knowing that light as fully as it is comprehended by God's Word and Spirit alone, but which all the same is so close and attainable that all of our blessedness lies in seeing God face to face.

Read Sheptytsky's words again. And this time, replace "holy" with "saint." How illuminating! But the exercise is not only instructive, it is essential. English is among the few languages that distinguish "saint" and "holy." In Greek, Latin, Slavonic—and a host of modern tongues—the two are the same word.

But the point is not linguistic, it is profoundly theological. We tend to reduce sanctity to good behavior. Of course, the two are inextricably related. Indeed, without the fruits of sanctity, there is no reason to venerate anyone. But how stultifying it is to overlook that holiness actually derives from union with the Holy One. How impoverishing to conceive of sanctity without first and foremost relating it to a depth that surpasses every conceivable thought. How limiting to forget that sanctity is ultimately a participation in inaccessible grandeur—nay transcendence and divine incomprehensibility!

Participating in the inaccessible is annoyingly paradoxical, but it is of such paradoxes that true life consists. Eastern Christianity revels in such "contradictions." Salvation, for example, is *theosis*—divinization. Humans become partakers of the divine nature (2 Peter 1:4). The sacraments—called "mysteries" in the East—are the very mystery of salvation. And certainly being a saint is about abiding in the holy.

But who is this Holy One? In our age of diverse spiritualities, it is easy to be tempted by mystical flights away from the real world of family and work, politics and pain. However, the Holy One who is raised from the fragmentation of hellish life is the one who descends into it. "You will not abandon my soul to the netherworld, nor will you suffer your holy one to see corruption" (Acts 2:27). It is on the cross, with its cry of abandonment, that Jesus, the Holy One of God, reveals God most powerfully. The saint is revealed in suffering and emerges victorious.

This brings us to what is certainly one of the more important contributions of J. Michael Thompson's wonderful book: the section devoted to the martyrs and confessors of the twentieth century. In my younger days, I would read the lives of the saints—the "classical" ones, that is—and think how imaginative the authors were in creating such gruesome accounts of torture. I knew the martyrs had really suffered, but I presumed that the references to foot spikes, flailing torture wheels, and boiling were embellishments.

And then I learned what had occurred only a few years before my birth in what the historian Timothy Snyder has labeled "the Bloodlands." Michael Thompson provides the vitae of Nicholas Charnetsky, Theodore Romzha, and Methodius Trcka. These represent a cross section that could be augmented with thousands of other modern lives from the Slavic crossroads of East and West. Many of those other saints, not included here, endured hardships that prove how unembellished the classical books on martyrs were. Indeed, Christians were boiled alive in the twentieth century! But this is not about the macabre. It is about hope. It is about the fact that it is possible to bear radical witness to Christ today in the modern world.

J. Michael Thompson's book—along with his earlier collection *Saints of the Roman Missal, Pray for Us*—certainly comes at an auspicious time. It seems we have transcended modern existentialism's aversion to imitation. Today, more and more young people seem willing to follow real heroes. My own experience, worshiping with university students on a regular basis, has revealed that the liturgical reading of the *Synaxarion* (a kind of Byzantine *Lives of the Saints*) is extremely popular. And recently, a thoroughly modern twenty-year-old told me that one of her favorite parts of Byzantine vespers is the hymns to the saints. "I love the details that vividly show what Christian living is about," she said.

This book is timely for another reason. Catholics worldwide are increasingly heeding the call of Pope John Paul II to breathe spiritually "with both lungs"—to be inspired by both Western and Eastern Christianity. In 1995 the pope wrote:

> *Since, in fact, we believe that the venerable and ancient tradition of the Eastern Churches is an integral part of the heritage of Christ's Church, the first need for Catholics is to be familiar with that tradition, so as to be nourished by it and to encourage the process of unity in the best way possible for each.*

> *Our Eastern Catholic brothers and sisters are very conscious of being the living bearers of this tradition, together with our Orthodox brothers and sisters. The members of the Catholic Church of the Latin tradition must also be fully acquainted with this treasure and thus feel, with the Pope, a passionate longing that*

the full manifestation of the Church's catholicity be restored to the Church and to the world, expressed not by a single tradition, and still less by one community in opposition to the other; and that we too may be granted a full taste of the divinely revealed and undivided heritage of the universal Church which is preserved and grows in the life of the Churches of the East as in those of the West.

APOSTOLIC LETTER ORIENTALE LUMEN, PARAGRAPH 1

The Holy Father speaks of the "process of unity" and that, with their Orthodox brothers and sisters, Eastern Catholics bear this dynamic Eastern tradition. It is apropos, then, to conclude with an "ode to unity" by another modern Eastern Catholic martyr, Fr. Omilian Kovch, who was sent to the Majdanek Nazi death camp for sheltering Jews. This is what he wrote to his wife and six children (Eastern Catholic priests can be married):

I understand that you are trying to get me released. But I beg you not to do this. Yesterday they killed fifty people. If I am not here, who will help them to get through these sufferings? [...]

I thank God for his goodness to me. Apart from heaven, this is the one place where I wish to remain. Here we are all equal: Poles, Jews, Ukrainians, Russians, Latvians, and Estonians. Of all these here, I am the only priest. I cannot even imagine how it would be here without me. Here I see God, who is the same for all of us, regardless of our religious distinctions. Perhaps our Churches are different, but the same great and Almighty God rules over us all. When I celebrate the Divine Liturgy, they all join in prayer [...]

They die in different ways, and I help them to cross over this little bridge into eternity. Is this not a blessing? Isn't this the greatest crown that God could have placed upon my head? It is indeed. I thank God a thousand times a day for sending me here. I do not ask him for anything else. Do not worry, and do not lose faith at what I share. Instead, rejoice with me.

Pray for those who created this concentration camp and this system. They are the only ones who need prayers. May God have mercy upon them.

In a world increasingly enamored of hatred, such odes to unity cannot be repeated often enough. But unity derives from love, and love from sacrifice. May the texts gathered in this book awaken a passion for the kinds of sacrifice offered by the saints fêted here. And may they stir us to always seek the Holy One. Indeed, to the question, "to whom shall we go?" Christ has the words of eternal life. We have believed, and have come to know, that he is the Holy One of God (see John 6:68–69)—the fully transcendent One, wholly in our midst.

Fr. Peter Galadza, PhD
Kule Family Professor of Liturgy
Metropolitan Andrey Sheptytsky Institute
of Eastern Christian Studies
Canada

INTRODUCTION

The drops of your blood, O Christ my God, together with the water that flowed from your side, have brought forth a new world; and they have gathered around you the divine assembly of all your saints.

TROPARION FROM ODE 6, CANON OF ALL SAINTS' SUNDAY

M any Catholics are unaware that the Roman Catholic Church is in communion with twenty-two other Churches, who together comprise the Eastern Catholic Churches. These Churches vary in rite (most are Byzantine, but some are Armenian, Syrian, Coptic, Ethiopian, and others). Geographically they originate from Central, Eastern, and Southern Europe; the Middle East; North Africa; and India. Some have branched out to other areas, including communicants in Western Europe, North America, South America, and Australia.

While all of these Churches (please note, not rites) are in communion with the pope of Rome, each has its own liturgy, its own canon law, its own spirituality.

This book attempts to share some of the saints of the Eastern Churches with readers. The saints featured in this book are on the calendar of three Eastern Churches: the Byzantine Catholic Church, whose American headquarters is in Pittsburgh; the Ukrainian Catholic Church, whose American headquarters is in Philadelphia; and the Melkite Catholic Church, whose American headquarters is in Newton, Massachusetts.

Lights From the East will open the incredible riches these saints offer the universal Church to English speakers worldwide. All of them are on the calendar in the *Liturgikon*, the official altar book of these Churches, and each is mentioned in the *Martyrologium Romanum*, the liturgical book that provides the official list of saints and blesseds for the Roman Catholic Church.

It is fitting to listen to the words of Pope John Paul II, who, in his Apostolic Letter *Orientale Lumen* (Light from the East), reflected in this way on the Eastern Christian experience face-to-face with the saints:

> *Today we often feel ourselves prisoners of the present. It is as though man had lost his perception of belonging to a history which precedes and follows him. This effort to situate oneself between the past and the future, with a grateful heart for the benefits received and for those expected, is offered by the Eastern Churches in particular, with a clear-cut sense of continuity which takes the name of Tradition and of eschatological expectation.*
>
> *Tradition is the heritage of Christ's Church. This is a living memory of the Risen One met and witnessed to by the Apostles who passed on his living memory to their successors in an uninterrupted line, guaranteed by the apostolic succession through the laying on of hands, down to the bishops of today. This is articulated in the historical and cultural patrimony of each Church, shaped by the witness of the martyrs, fathers and saints, as well as by the living faith of all Christians down the centuries to our own day. It is not an unchanging repetition of formulas, but a heritage which preserves its original, living, kerygmatic core. It is Tradition that preserves the Church from the danger of gathering only changing opinions, and guarantees her certitude and continuity.*

Each entry in this book provides:

- An icon of the saint(s)
- A biography or biographies
- A Scripture passage
- A quotation from the *Menaion** service in honor of the saint (complete sources of the quotations are on page 144)
- A spiritual reflection
- A prayer
- A hymn to the saint, set to a Rusyn or Galician melody

This format will help readers become familiar with the featured saints, and enable them to allow the saints to enter their own prayer life. The saints range from biblical heroes or martyrs of the early Church to those who gave their lives serving the Eastern Catholic Churches during Soviet persecution. All of these saints remained faithful to their own Church while maintaining communion with the See of Rome.

* The *Menaion* is the twelve-volume work that gives the hymnody, prayers, and readings honoring each saint on the Byzantine calendar.

SECTION I

SAINTS OF THE
OLD AND NEW TESTAMENTS

THREE HOLY YOUTHS

PROPHET DANIEL

Ananias, Azariah, and Mishael are the Hebrew
names of the Three Young Men, as rendered by the
Septuagint version of the Old Testament used for
centuries in the Eastern Churches and still used today.
The names Shadrach, Meshach, and Abednego—
the names found in the Book of Daniel—are
Babylonian names that were imposed on them
during their exile.

FR. MAREK VISNOVSKY

I

THE HOLY PROPHET DANIEL AND THE THREE HOLY YOUTHS

Feast Day: December 17

The first layer of saints in the calendar features the worthies of the Bible. In both the Eastern and Western calendars, there are multiple commemorations from both the Old and New Testaments. In the Eastern Churches, however, rather than just being listed on the calendar, these holy men and women have commemoration services in their honor.

On December 17, the Byzantine Churches remember the prophet Daniel and his companions Ananias, Azariah, and Mishael (the Greek forms of their names), otherwise known as "the Three Young Men." Daniel is the fourth of the major prophets.

The Book of Daniel provides information about both the prophet and the youths. These men were Israelites carried away into Babylon after the Babylonian army conquered and destroyed the city of Jerusalem. They were taken into the service of King Nebuchadnezzar, who ordered them to serve at his table. During this time, they maintained the dietary rules of the Torah. Their loyalty to the God of Israel caused them all to be condemned: the Three Young Men to the fiery furnace and Daniel to the lions' den. In all of their tribulations, the Lord stood by them and rescued them from their perils. Having overcome the horrendous events with the assistance of the God of Israel, each survived and received places of honor in the Babylonian court.

More than many Old Testament saints, Daniel and the Three Young Men are a particularly vivid part of the Byzantine Church's memory. The Seventh and Eighth Odes (biblical canticles) sung in the Byzantine Office of Matins are both taken from the Book of the prophet Daniel. And most of the poetic material used with those canticles will refer to events from the lives of the Three Young Men in the fiery furnace.

SCRIPTURE

Then King Nebuchadnezzar was startled and rose in haste, asking his counselors, "Did we not cast three men bound into the fire?" "Certainly, O king," they answered.

"But," he replied, "I see four men unbound and unhurt, walking in the fire, and the fourth looks like a son of God."

Then Nebuchadnezzar came to the opening of the white-hot furnace and called: "Shadrach, Meshach, and Abednego, servants of the Most High God, come out." Thereupon Shadrach, Meshach, and Abednego came out of the fire.

When the satraps, prefects, governors, and counselors of the king came together, they saw that the fire had had no power over the bodies of these men; not a hair of their heads had been singed, nor were their garments altered; there was not even a smell of fire about them.

Nebuchadnezzar exclaimed, "Blessed be the God of Shadrach, Meshach, and Abednego, who sent his angel to deliver the servants that trusted in him; they disobeyed the royal command and yielded their bodies rather than serve or worship any god except their own God.

DANIEL 3:91–95

QUOTATION

Great are the deeds performed with faith:

Three youths rejoiced in the flaming furnace

As if they stood in refreshing waters;

And Daniel the prophet faced lions as though they were sheep.

Through their prayers, O Christ our God, save our souls!

Troparion, Tone 2

REFLECTION

Both the prophet Daniel and the Three Young Men demonstrate for us the necessity of maintaining our fidelity to God, no matter what circumstances or difficulties arise. This applies to what we say, but it also is true for the way we live our lives. We are called to be faithful both in word and in action.

PRAYER

All glory to you, O Christ our God, who gave wisdom to your prophets and strengthened the Three Young Men and the prophet Daniel in their exile in Babylon with courage to keep your law unblemished from corruption or defilement. Through your Spirit, you gave Daniel the ability to interpret dreams and to give wise counsel. Through the hymns of the Three Young Men, your Church is given words to praise you in your creation. Grant that we, nourished by their words and challenged by their actions, may be a people of praise and conviction, fearlessly giving you glory in all your works and testimony of you in our daily lives. May we glorify you with your Father who has no beginning and your all-holy Spirit, now and ever and forever. Amen.

HYMN

As a star, resplendent, announces the break of day,
We praise you, O Daniel, who prophesied Messiah's way.
　　As the feast approaches, we are filled with gladness!
　　Hear Your saints, O Master, who join us as we pray.
Through the fiery furnace, O youths, you blessed your fathers' God.
Heedless of temptation, in purity God's path you trod.
　　As the feast approaches, we are filled with gladness!
　　Hear Your saints, O Master, who join us as we pray.
Fortified by fasting, Your holy ones were bold and brave,
Kept safe by You, Lord God, who show Yourself as strong to save!
　　As the feast approaches, we are filled with gladness!
　　Hear Your saints, O Master, who join us as we pray.

TUNE: *PRIZRI, O MARIJE / MARY, LOOK UPON US*
TEXT: J. MICHAEL THOMPSON

A hymn for the Prophet Daniel and the Three Young Men

tune: Prizri, O Marije / Mary, Look Upon Us
source: traditional Carpatho-Rusyn melody

1. As a star, re - splen-dent, an - noun - ces the break of day,
2. Through the fi - ery fur - nace, O youths, you blessed your fa - thers' God.
3. For - ti - fied by fast - ing, Your ho - ly ones were bold and brave,

We praise you, O Dan - iel, who pro - phe - sied Mes - si - ah's way.
Heed - less of temp - ta - tion, in pu - ri - ty God's path you trod.
Kept safe by You, Lord God, who show Your-self as strong to save!

Refrain

As the feast ap - proach-es, we are filled with glad-ness!

Hear Your saints, O Mas - ter, who join us as we pray.

© 2013, J. Michael Thompson

SAINT THEKLA

القديسة تقلا

PROTO- MARTYR

Protomartyr: The first martyr
in a cause

FR. ELIAS RAFAJ

II

THE HOLY FIRST-MARTYR AND EQUAL-TO-THE-APOSTLES THECLA

Feast Day: September 24

B orn in the city of Iconium, Thecla, sometimes spelled "Thekla," according to tradition was the daughter of wealthy and influential parents and was renowned, from a young age, for her good looks. As was the norm at the time, when she reached eighteen her parents arranged her engagement to a young man of the city. Thecla, however, had heard St. Paul the Apostle preaching about Jesus Christ, which prompted her to decide never to marry. She decided to follow the apostles' example, giving herself to preaching the Good News of Jesus. In part as a result of this, Paul was arrested by the city authorities and was exiled from Iconium.

After Paul left the city, Thecla's parents pressed her to agree to be married, but this had no effect on the young woman. Her mother wept bitterly with her and had her dragged before the city magistrate to be threatened with torture. In the face of all this opposition, Thecla received baptism and publicly professed Jesus Christ. This action provoked the municipal authorities to try to put her to death, but the attempts were thwarted by divine intervention.

Thecla left Iconium, proceeding to the city of Antioch. There she joined the Apostles Paul and Barnabas, who were preaching and building up the Christian community there. It was in Antioch that the followers of Jesus were first called "Christians." After a certain amount of time, with the permission and direction of Paul, Thecla moved to the region of Isaurian Seleucia, which was very remote from city life. She lived there a long time, teaching the local people about Jesus Christ. She was renowned for her ability to cure those who were ill by praying with them. Through her tireless work there, many came to believe in Christ. For this labor, the Church gave her the title of "equal-to-the-apostles," a term of honor reserved for those who converted nations to Christianity.

When Thecla was about ninety, her healing ministry became an affront to certain of the pagan priests in that area. She endeavored to convince them that any healing on her part was actually done through the power of Jesus Christ. This caused them to be jealous of her. In their attempt to discredit her, her enemies sent men to rape her and dishonor her connection to Christ. As the men approached her, Thecla called out to her Lord and asked to be delivered. A large stone split open and took her life, preserving her from their evil intentions. Thecla is called a "protomartyr" because she is the first woman who witnessed to Christ with her life's blood. Many churches in the Byzantine East are dedicated to her. In the city of Constantinople, a famous church was erected by the Emperor St. Constantine the Great (yet another who bears the title "equal-to-the-apostles"). To this day, Thecla is considered a powerful help for all of those living the monastic life in its bodily rigor, and her name is among the saints who are invoked during the rite of tonsuring, the introductory action bringing people into the monastic state.

SCRIPTURE

Now in regard to virgins, I have no commandment from the Lord, but I give my opinion as one who by the Lord's mercy is trustworthy.

So this is what I think best because of the present distress: that it is a good thing for a person to remain as he is.

Are you bound to a wife? Do not seek a separation. Are you free of a wife? Then do not look for a wife.

If you marry, however, you do not sin, nor does an unmarried woman sin if she marries; but such people will experience affliction in their earthly life, and I would like to spare you that.

I tell you, brothers, the time is running out. From now on, let those having wives act as not having them,

those weeping as not weeping, those rejoicing as not rejoicing, those buying as not owning,

those using the world as not using it fully. For the world in its present form is passing away.

I should like you to be free of anxieties. An unmarried man is anxious about the things of the Lord, how he may please the Lord.

But a married man is anxious about the things of the world, how he may please his wife,

and he is divided. An unmarried woman or a virgin is anxious about the things of the Lord, so that she may be holy in both body and spirit. A married woman, on the other hand, is anxious about the things of the world, how she may please her husband.

I am telling you this for your own benefit, not to impose a restraint upon you, but for the sake of propriety and adherence to the Lord without distraction.

1 CORINTHIANS 7:25–35

QUOTATION

Inspired by the divine teacher's words,

you were inflamed with love for your Creator.

you disdained all earthly pleasures

And endured wild beasts and fire.

O glorious Thecla, companion of Paul,

Entreat your divine Bridegroom

To grant us His great mercy.

TROPARION, TONE 4

REFLECTION

Once we have heard the call of the Lord, other things no longer take first place in our lives. The ties of family love, which are good and holy, are still secondary to the will of God for our lives and must be treated as such. The life of St. Thecla also reminds us that societal restrictions (that is, "you cannot do this or that because you are a woman, a young person, etc.") are also to be viewed—and, if necessary, disregarded—in light of the will of the Lord for us.

PRAYER

O Christ, you are the Bridegroom of your holy Church. You have called countless men and women to follow you, for you are the Way, the Truth and the Life. We give you thanks for the witness of your saints throughout the ages who have responded to your command to "come, follow me!" We especially thank you for your handmaid Thecla, who heard the preaching of your Apostles Paul and Barnabas and gave up home and family to carry your Good News to the nations. In the face of disdain and fierce persecution, she joyfully shared your word with everyone she met and was faithful to you despite torture and violent death, imitating you, her Master and Redeemer. May her example strengthen us to share your love and truth with all around us so the world may know you, the one sent by the Father and testified to by the Holy Spirit, one God through ages unending. Amen.

HYMN

God of grace, whose mercy calls us:
"Come and follow!"
Hear the anthem that we raise You,
Take the song with which we praise You
For this Your saint, Thecla.

Having heard Your Gospel gracious,
"Come and follow!"
Thecla, urged by Paul's strong preaching,
Told Your love, new souls now reaching.
We praise Your saint, Thecla.

Through her martyr's death she urges,
"Come and follow!"
Father, Son, and Spirit praising,
We will tell Your grace amazing
Given Your saint, Thecla.

TUNE: *PRENEBESNA, PRECHUDESNA* / *QUEEN OF HEAVEN* (GALICIAN)
TEXT: J. MICHAEL THOMPSON

A hymn for the Holy First-Martyr Thecla

tune: Prenebesna, Prechudesna / Queen of Heaven
author: J. Duts'ko (20th century)

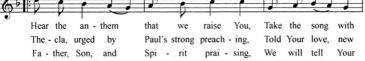

1. God of grace, whose mer - cy calls us: "Come and fol - low!"
2. Hav - ing heard Your Gos - pel gra - cious, "Come and fol - low!"
3. Through her mar - tyr's death she ur - ges, "Come and fol - low!"

Hear the an - them that we raise You, Take the song with
The - cla, urged by Paul's strong preach - ing, Told Your love, new
Fa - ther, Son, and Spi - rit prai - sing, We will tell Your

which we praise You For this Your saint, The - cla.
souls now reach - ing. We praise Your saint, The - cla.
grace a - maz - ing Gi - ven Your saint, The - cla.

© 2013, J. Michael Thompson

SECTION II

✥

PERIOD OF THE
FATHERS, MOTHERS,
AND MARTYRS

SAINT BARBARA

The **"Fourteen Holy Helpers,"** all saints, were popularly invoked in the West against the plague and other serious difficulties. St. Barbara was invoked against "sudden and unprepared-for death."

FR. ELIAS RAFAJ

III

THE HOLY GREAT-MARTYR BARBARA

Feast Day: December 4

The Church of Antioch in Syria is the cradle of many martyrs. The holy great-martyr Barbara is one of the most beloved in that group of witnesses to Christ. Her fame traveled from east to west, where St. Barbara was invoked during the Middle Ages and thereafter as one of the "Fourteen Holy Helpers."

Most texts on the lives of the early saints, rather than giving a year descriptor in numbers, will talk about the reign of a given Roman emperor. So the hagiographies about Barbara tell us she was born during the reign of Emperor Maximian (circa 286–305) to wealthy pagan parents in Heliopolis, Syria. Her father was Dioscorus, who lost his wife soon after Barbara's birth. His daughter became his pride and joy and the focus of much of his attention after his wife's death.

Being aware that his daughter was beautiful beyond the ordinary, he tried to keep her from interacting with neighbors. On his property, he had a tower constructed. Barbara lived in the tower and was permitted contact only with servants and tutors. The tower provided Barbara with an incredibly lovely vista, and she feasted on the sight both day and night. As she grew, Barbara reflected upon this beauty, wondering about the source that had provided such loveliness and order. The more she reflected upon these things, the greater was her assurance that the gods that her father and her tutors worshiped were not capable of such wonders. Her yearning to encounter the true power behind the universe grew stronger each day.

Meanwhile, Barbara's reputation for being a beautiful young lady spread in her city, and soon there was a line of suitors who sought her father's permission to marry his daughter. Barbara, however, was not interested in granting the wishes of any of them. She told her father that his continued efforts to marry her off would not come to a good end. He, however, thought that the isolation in which he had kept Barbara had caused her to fear strangers. In hopes of changing her mind, he freed her from her isolation in the tower, permitting her to associate with people from the city. It was in this way that Barbara met for the first time Christian women and girls. And through them her intense desire to know about the source of creation was granted.

These Christian women and girls taught Barbara about the one God who made the entire world and about God's self-revelation as a Trinity-in-unity, Father, Son, and Holy Spirit, and, of course about Jesus Christ. Around this time, a Christian priest arrived in her city, traveling from Alexandria in Egypt under the alias of a merchant. After completing the instruction in the Christian faith that her friends had begun, he brought her to the mysteries of initiation (Baptism, Chrismation, and Eucharist). When next she saw her father, she professed Christ publicly. This caused her father to become enraged at her, and he went to the civil authorities. They arrested her and subjected her to vile torture.

The torture of Barbara was done in a public place in order to drive fear into the hearts of the citizens so they would either denounce Christ or at least see that being a Christian was not worth their lives. One of the people in the crowd was a Christian woman named Juliana. She was moved by the witness of this young woman who refused to deny her Lord and Savior. Responding to their brutal treatment of Barbara, Juliana started to rebuke the torturers and confessed her own belief in Christ. She, too, was apprehended by the authorities and put to the same sort of sufferings. These included being attacked with hooks, followed by being carried naked while the crowds mocked and scorned them. Barbara prayed that they might not be shamed before the crowds, and in answer an angel came and provided a glorious garment to cover them. Finally, faithful to the end, Barbara and Juliana were killed by decapitation.

A while after her death, the holy relics of Barbara were transmitted to the imperial city of Constantinople. Much later, they went to Kiev with Princess Barbara, the daughter of the Byzantine Emperor Alexius Comnenus, who arranged her marriage to the prince of Kievan Rus', Michael Izyaslavich. To this day, these relics are venerated in the Cathedral of St. Volodymyr the Great in the city of Kiev. While the primary feast of the holy virgin martyr is kept on December 4, the feast of the translation of her relics is kept on July 11.

SCRIPTURE

Consider your own calling, brothers. Not many of you were wise by human standards, not many were powerful, not many were of noble birth.

Rather, God chose the foolish of the world to shame the wise, and God chose the weak of the world to shame the strong,

and God chose the lowly and despised of the world, those who count for nothing, to reduce to nothing those who are something,

so that no human being might boast before God.

It is due to him that you are in Christ Jesus, who became for us wisdom from God, as well as righteousness, sanctification, and redemption,

so that, as it is written, "Whoever boasts, should boast in the Lord."

1 CORINTHIANS 1:26–31

QUOTATION

O honorable and triumphant Barbara,

you believed in the Holy Trinity,

And renounced the multiplicity of pagan deities.

you fought for your faith with great courage,

And were not frightened by threats of your persecutors,

But declared instead in a clear voice:

"I adore one God in three Divine Persons."

KONTAKION, TONE 4

REFLECTION

The mystery of the Holy Trinity—one God in three divine persons—is fundamental to the Christian faith. As the hymnody for St. Barbara states, it was faith in the Trinity and in the Incarnation of our Lord Jesus Christ that led the saint to her bold witness ("martyr" is Greek for "witness"), confirming her faith with her life's blood. The next time you make the Sign of the Cross, give thanks to God for this saving faith.

PRAYER

O Christ, second person of the holy and undivided Trinity, you are the icon of the invisible God. Through your Incarnation, you have brought the life of the Godhead into contact with the human race, and through your ascension, you have taken humanity back with you to the heavenly realm. By asking the Father, he has sent the Holy Spirit, the Paraclete, into our hearts that we might be temples of your glory. Hear our prayer of thanksgiving, which we offer for the life and witness of your handmaiden Barbara. From her youth, she sought the truth of life that was revealed to her through the Gospel. Once exposed to you, she became your devoted servant, giving her whole self over to you. When threatened by her father and the governor, she remained committed to you and refused to deny you, even at the cost of her own life. Through your grace, help us to love you as she did and to live our lives rooted in you, O Lord. For you are our God, and we give glory to you, O Christ, with your Father who is without beginning, and your all-holy and life-giving Spirit, now and ever and forever. Amen.

HYMN

Loving God, whose service calls forth
Courage in Your servant's soul,
We here gathered sing the praise of
One who bravely reached heav'n's goal.
Claiming Christ as only Savior,
Scorning those with evil planned,
Now with white-robed brilliance vested,
Near your throne she finds her stand.

Teach us, as You taught St. Barb'ra,
How to love and serve Your Name
That our hearts may not be conquered
By our fears or love of fame.
As she loved You to her last breath,
Give us strength to faithful be,
That our witness may be fearless
And our lives unfeigned and free.

Glory be to God, the Father,
Glory be to God, the Son,
Glory be to God, the Spirit:
Glory to the Three-in-One!
From the virgin choirs of heaven
And from tempted saints below,
Endless hymns and praise unceasing
Shall from all our hearts e'er flow.

TUNE: *O God's Mother*
TEXT: J. MICHAEL THOMPSON

A hymn for the Holy Great-Martyr Barbara

tune: O God's Mother
author: J. Michael Thompson (2005)

1. Lov-ing God, whose ser-vice calls forth cour-age in Your ser-vant's soul, We here ga-thered sing the praise of One who brave-ly reached heav'n's goal. Claim-ing Christ as on-ly Sa-vior, Scorn-ing those with e-vil planned, Now with white-robed bril-liance vest-ed, Near Your throne she finds her stand.

2. Teach us, as You taught St. Bar-b'ra, How to love and serve Your Name That our hearts may not be con-quered By our fears or love of fame. As she loved You to her last breath, Give us strength to faith-ful be, That our wit-ness may be fear-less And our lives un-feigned and free.

3. Glo-ry be to God, the Fa-ther, Glo-ry be to God, the Son, Glo-ry be to God, the Spi-rit: Glo-ry to the Three-in-One! From the vir-gin choirs of hea-ven And from tempt-ed saints be-low, End-less hymns and praise un-ceas-ing Shall from all our hearts e'er flow.

© 2013, J. Michael Thompson

SAI
N
T

MAC
RI
NA

FR. ELIAS RAFAJ

Macrina was renowned for being
able to do amazing things in God's
name and so was nicknamed
"the wonder worker."

IV

OUR VENERABLE
MOTHER MACRINA
THE YOUNGER

Feast Day: July 19

We often talk about things like hair color or the shape of certain facial features as running in a family. In the family of St. Macrina the Younger, we could observe that sanctity was a dominant characteristic of her family. She was born in the province of Cappadocia sometime around 330 to the devout Christian couple Basil and Emilia. They named her for her grandmother. She was one of nine offspring. From that family, the grandmother (St. Macrina the Elder), the parents (St. Basil and St. Emilia), and three of her brothers (St. Basil the Great, St. Gregory of Nyssa, and St. Peter of Sebaste) are all honored along with her as saints of the Church.

Trained by her mother, St. Emilia, Macrina was brought up in a strict and wholesome Christian environment. She learned to read and write using the books of holy Scripture and the Psalter, providing the young girl with the pattern of a life holy and pleasing to God. She was also guided by her grandmother and mother to manage the family household, which included cooking, cleaning, weaving, and many other practical tasks.

When she was sixteen, she was engaged to a young man of a similar Christian background but who died before the marriage was consummated. When her father tried to have her arrange another marriage, she declined, making the choice to vow herself to Christ as a virgin remaining in her family home. Macrina aided her parents by acting as steward of the family estate. She was instrumental in the raising of her younger brothers and sisters in the same sort of pious rearing that she had experienced.

Once her siblings left home, Macrina persuaded her mother to make a decision to enter into monastic life with her and several of their servants. They ended up living together in a new form of family, where prayer, work, and possessions were all in common, and where social status was set aside for the sake of the community. Upon the passing of her mother, Macrina became the new "mother" of the community.

In a time when Christians were often very critical of one another, her reputation was held in high esteem by all who had heard of her. She was known for her personal ascetic behavior as well as for her gentleness with those she governed. Macrina came to be renowned for her ability to do amazing things in God's name and so was nicknamed "the wonder worker." She reposed in the Lord in 379, giving thanks to God for the gifts she had received from him. Some of the things she said on her deathbed were reported by her saintly brothers Basil and Gregory in their writings. Her body was laid to rest in the same tomb that contained the bodies of her father and mother.

SCRIPTURE

For this reason I kneel before the Father,

from whom every family in heaven and on earth is named,

that he may grant you in accord with the riches of his glory to be strengthened with power through his Spirit in the inner self,

and that Christ may dwell in your hearts through faith; that you, rooted and grounded in love,

may have strength to comprehend with all the holy ones what is the breadth and length and height and depth,

and to know the love of Christ that surpasses knowledge, so that you may be filled with all the fullness of God.

Now to him who is able to accomplish far more than all we ask or imagine, by the power at work within us,

to him be glory in the church and in Christ Jesus to all generations, forever and ever. Amen.

EPHESIANS 3:14–21

QUOTATION

You loved the good God with all your heart, O Macrina.

You shouldered your cross and sincerely followed him.

You found the total remission of your sins in him.

KONTAKION, TONE 4

REFLECTION

The Christian family is the place where faith in Christ is nourished and encouraged, and love for others is implanted there in us from our youngest days. St. Macrina grew up in such a family and took that family as a model for the monastic life she lived with such devotion. How are our households a reflection of Christ's love for others?

PRAYER

O Christ, who dwell in the community of love that is the Holy Trinity, we thank you for the witness of countless women and men who have gathered and formed households of faith. We thank you for our families, the home churches that have cradled true life in us while preparing us for a life of holiness. We also thank you for those monastic, religious, and lay leaders whose family lives overflowed into a life of service for our communities as they centered themselves on you.

You filled Macrina with knowledge and reverence for you from her earliest days through those within her own family, who set an example of holiness for her. She dedicated herself to a monastic life in you and encouraged her brothers in their episcopal ministry to serve your holy people. Looking to Macrina as our model, we ask that you grant us, your people, the grace to entrust our whole lives to you. For you, O Christ, are the Savior of all peoples. We glorify you, Jesus, with the Father and the Holy Spirit, now and forever. Amen.

HYMN

Come, all you faithful
With hymns most holy
Bring to Christ Jesus
Songs full of glory,
Giving God thanks profound on this day
That this, our sister, has walked His way.

In good Macrina,
God's own perfection
Bids us to follow
Her with affection.
Living the common life faithfully,
Knowing the narrow way sets us free.

Glory to Father,
Son, and dear Spirit,
Trinity loving!
Let us inherit,
With Saint Macrina, when time shall cease,
Life everlasting, Your heav'n of peace.

TUNE: *MARIYE DIVO / VIRGIN MOST BLESSED*

TEXT: J. MICHAEL THOMPSON

A hymn for our Venerable Mother Macrina

tune: Mariye Divo / Virgin Most Blessed
source: "Tserkovni pisni," 1926

1. Come, all you faith - ful With hymns most ho - ly
2. In good Ma - cri - na, God's own per - fec - tion
3. Glo - ry to Fa - ther, Son, and dear Spi - rit,

Bring to Christ Je - sus Songs full of glo - ry,
Bids us to fol - low Her with af - fec - tion.
Tri - ni - ty lov - ing! Let us in - her - it,

Giv - ing God thanks pro - found on this day
Liv - ing the com - mon life faith - ful - ly,
With Saint Ma - cri - na, when time shall cease,

That this, our sis - ter, has walked His way.
Know - ing the nar - row way sets us free.
Life e - ver - last - ing, Your heav'n of peace.

© 2013, J. Michael Thompson

Ὁ Γ Ἅ Ι Ο Σ CÁBBAC

He who loves God foregoes the fleeting to possess knowledge of Him.

Sabbas was dedicated to the **Orthodox** teachings about the two natures of Christ and preached adamantly against the Monophysite heresy that was infecting the Church in his day.

FR. ELIAS RAFAJ

V

OUR VENERABLE FATHER SABBAS THE SANCTIFIED

Feast Day: December 5

Sometimes in reading history, we encounter a person who affects our own life experience and immediately wonder, "Why didn't I know of him or her?" Sabbas (sometimes spelled "Sava") is one of those people.

The story of Sabbas begins in the fifth century in the village of Mutalaska, in the province of Cappadocia. His parents were John, a commander in the Roman army, and Sophia. They were people of good Christian reputation. When young Sabbas was five, his father went on assignment to Alexandria. His wife accompanied him, but they decided to commit their son to the care of his uncle. Three years later, Sabbas entered St. Flavian Monastery, which was close to his uncle's home. It took very little time in the monastery for Sabbas to learn to read. His elders were amazed at the way he mastered the Scriptures, committing much of them to memory. His parents tried to persuade him to leave the monastery and marry, but Sabbas had found his vocation.

Sabbas entered the monastic estate at the age of seventeen, when he was tonsured by the abbot. He was recognized by his community as a model of prayer and bodily discipline, and God's blessing on the young monk was manifested by the gift of "wonder working" (that is, the working of miracles). After ten years as a monk in Cappadocia, he received his abbot's blessing to move to the monastery in Jerusalem headed by St. Euthymius the Great. Upon Sabbas' arrival, St. Euthymius directed him to another monastic elder, Abba Theoctistus. It was in this community, which observed the discipline of life in common with great rigor, that Sabbas lived. He was noted for his observance of the Rule and thrived there until he was thirty years old.

When Abba Theoctistus fell asleep in the Lord, Sabbas was given the blessing by the new abbot that he might live in solitude in a nearby cave. This was seen as the "next step" in monastic practice, which not everyone attained. He would, however, return to the larger community for the liturgical services and communal meals on Saturdays and Sundays. Eventually, Sabbas was permitted by his abbot to remain alone in his cave. The cave became his place of spiritual warfare for five years.

During this time, Sabbas was under the watchful eye of St. Euthymius the Great. Observing his growth in the spiritual life, the elder took him into the wilderness, and the two of them remained there between mid-January and Flowery Sunday (Palm Sunday). It was St. Euthymius who gave Sabbas the title of "child elder," and his counsel guided the young monk as he developed in living the difficult monastic life.

In 473, St. Euthymius reposed. At that time, Sabbas left the monastery, going from there to the Monastery of St. Gerasimus near the Jordan River. He settled there in a remote cave. Despite his attempt to be solitary, his way of life attracted men to him. These men wanted to follow Sabbas and his vision of the life of a monk. Eventually, the number of men with him grew enough that a cenobium (a place where monks lived in community, rather than as isolated hermits) was founded there.

It was at this monastery that Sabbas compiled the first monastic Rule of church services, which came to be known either as the "Jerusalem Typikon" or the "St. Sabbas Typikon," which came to be followed by the monks and nuns living in the communities of Palestine.

Sabbas was dedicated to the Orthodox teachings about the two natures of our Lord Jesus Christ and preached adamantly against the Monophysite heresy that was infecting the Church at that time. This actually got him to leave his beloved monastery so he might urge the emperor to defend the true faith.

His nickname "the Sanctified" is believed to come from his ordination to the priesthood. This was accomplished by the patriarch of Jerusalem, Salustius, in 491. It was Patriarch Salustius who appointed him as the monastic head or supervisor of the monks of Palestine. This permitted his typikon to have immense influence on Byzantine Christian liturgical life.

In the year 532, surrounded by his monastic sons, Sabbas fell asleep in the Lord.

SCRIPTURE

My son, if you receive my words
and treasure my commands,

Turning your ear to wisdom,
inclining your heart to understanding;

Yes, if you call for intelligence,
and to understanding raise your voice;

If you seek her like silver,
and like hidden treasures search her out,

Then will you understand the fear of the LORD;
the knowledge of God you will find;

For the LORD *gives wisdom,*
from his mouth come knowledge and understanding.

PROVERBS 2:1–6

QUOTATION

From your youth, O glorious Sabbas,

You have been like an offering of incense in God's presence.

You were called an adornment of hermits

And a true ascetic.

Therefore, we cry out to you:

"Rejoice, O Father, worthy of all praise!"

KONTAKION, TONE 8

REFLECTION

Obedience is currently a profoundly unpopular virtue. It is seen as the opposite of freedom from the spirit of this world. The life of St. Sabbas testifies to a scriptural understanding of obedience as an act where one surrenders his or her free will to God, allowing this virtue to become the foundation of a fruitful life in Christ. Sabbas' life also exemplifies the spiritual life in Eastern Christian understanding. If one is serious about life in God, it is necessary for guidance to be given by a spiritual father or mother. Am I trying to go it alone, or am I seriously trying to find mature guidance for my life in Christ?

PRAYER

O Christ, you went into the wilderness and prayed to your Father, setting an example for your people to follow. We thank you for St. Sabbas the Sanctified, who fled the world so he could find you. His life was hidden in God and became a shining light both for the people of his age and for the people who have followed. Through his example, teach us to willingly accept poverty and hardship so we might be singly focused on doing your holy will in our lives. May his love and daily praise teach us to worship you at all times and in all places, giving thanks for all the good you do for us. Through St. Sabbas' memorization of the word of God, may we be led to feed ever more fully on you, the living Word and Bread come down from heaven. Glory to you, O Christ, the Light of your people, to the Father without end, and the all-holy and life-giving Spirit, now and ever and forever. Amen.

HYMN

O father of th' angelic life,
And fellow of the saints,
You have your dwelling now with Christ
The Goal of your restraint.
O light of temp'rance, monks' defense,
We honor you each year;
Pray to the Christ who was your Light,
That we be saved from fear.

As you, through discipline, restored
The flesh for Spirit's task,
So guide us now who look to you,
Each deadly sin unmask.
Pray for all monks and nuns this day
That they might heed God's call,
And for the folk who sing your praise,
That they give God their all.

In midst of winter fast and prayer
We raise our song of praise
To Father, Son, and Spirit, God,
Who blesses all our days.
As we prepare for Christmas now,
Give us the grace to grow
In knowledge and in love of You,
That we Your grace may show!

TUNE: *POD TVOJ POKROV* / *WE HASTEN*
TEXT: J. MICHAEL THOMPSON

A hymn for our Venerable Father Sabbas the Sanctified

tune: Pod tvoj pokrov / We Hasten
source: Užhorod "Pisennik" (1913)

1. O fa - ther of th'an - gel - ic life, And fel - low
2. As you, through di - sci - pline, re - stored The flesh for
3. In midst of win - ter fast and prayer We raise our

of the saints, You have your dwel - ling now with
Spi - rit's task, So guide us now who look to
song of praise To Fa - ther, Son, and Spi - rit,

Christ The Goal of your re - straint.
you, Each dead - ly sin un - mask.
God, Who bles - ses all our days.

O light of tem - p'rance, monks' de - fense, We
Pray for all monks and nuns this day That
As we pre - pare for Christ - mas now, Give

hon - or you each year; Pray to the Christ who
they might heed God's call, And for the folk who
us the grace to grow In know - ledge and in

was your Light, That we be saved from fear.
sing your praise, That they give God their all.
love of You, That we Your grace may show!

© 2006, J. Michael Thompson

SAINT MARIA

SAINT XENO-PHON

FR. ELIAS RAFAJ

The brothers Arcadius and John, sons of Xenophon and Mary, were victims of a disaster when their ship was destroyed at sea. A surprising turn of events then transpired.

VI

VENERABLE XENOPHON AND MARY, AND THEIR SONS, ARCADIUS AND JOHN

Feast Day: January 26

On January 26, the Byzantine Churches celebrate the feast of an entire family: father Xenophon, mother Maria, and their two sons, Arcadius and John. Living in the fifth century in the city of Constantinople, Xenophon was a member of the Imperial Senate. The family was socially prominent and wealthy but was more renowned for their austere lifestyle and love for the poor and needy. When both sons reached an age where they could leave home to receive advanced education, the parents had them journey by sea to Beirut in Philistia, where they were to attend school.

The brothers were victims of a disaster when the ship on which they traveled was destroyed. In the stormy Mediterranean Sea, the two men were alienated, both reaching shore but separated from each other. Arcadius ended up south of the city of Tyre and John at the city of Melphytan. Unaware that the other had survived the shipwreck, each brother sought out a monastery and joined that community. News of the shipwreck eventually reached the parents in Constantinople with no news of their sons. Family friends consoled them, believing the sons had been lost at sea.

While trying to comfort Maria, Xenophon was confident that God had preserved the lives of their sons. After a few years, a bishop blessed the couple prior to them making their pilgrimage to the Holy Land. While in Jerusalem, they went to the Church of the Holy Sepulchre. There in the city of Jerusalem they were surprised and delighted to encounter both sons, who had also made a pilgrimage from their respective monasteries.

The whole family went to the Monastery of Mar Saba near Jerusalem to make some important decisions. Xenophon wrote a letter to the capital, resigning from his senatorial position and handing over his power of attorney to a friend with instructions to sell all the family's property and distribute the proceeds to the poor. Xenophon and his sons asked to be taken in as members of the community at Mar Saba, and Maria went to a separate women's monastery nearby. The grace of God was made evident in the lives of all four members of the family, who had become joyfully reunited through God's love and mercy.

SCRIPTURE

Consider it all joy, my brothers, when you encounter various trials,

for you know that the testing of your faith produces perseverance.

And let perseverance be perfect, so that you may be perfect and complete, lacking in nothing.

But if any of you lacks wisdom, he should ask God who gives to all generously and ungrudgingly, and he will be given it.

But he should ask in faith, not doubting, for the one who doubts is like a wave of the sea that is driven and tossed about by the wind.

JAMES 1:2–6

QUOTATION

You were attentive to the commandments of the Master,
Distributing your wealth secretly to the poor, O blessed one,
With your wife and children.
Therefore, you dwell in the divine paradise.

KONTAKION, TONE 4

REFLECTION

The exemplar for the life of husband and wife is the relationship that Christ has with his Church. True conjugal love will be shown in the ability to live and love sacrificially and in the ability to do so with a joyful spirit. God's grace provides couples with the gift to accomplish this, bestowed in the mystery of holy crowning (known in the Western Church as the sacrament of holy matrimony). It is this sacrificial love that then leads to the bearing and rearing of children with love and fear of the Lord. How are we living out the promises and commitments we have made?

PRAYER

O Christ, in your self-giving unto death, you modeled the relationship between husband and wife for your people, and in your sanctification of the wedding at Cana of Galilee raised the divinely instituted marriage of man and woman to one of your Church's sacred mysteries.

We thank you for the witness of your saints Xenophon and Maria, and their sons Arcadius and John. In all of their tribulations, they remained faithful to you, and when relieved of their difficulties, they turned to you in praise and thanksgiving. Give grace to all who are living in the mystery of holy crowning, that their lives and their love may be a testimony to your love and peace in their lives. All glory to you, O Christ, living in the bond of unending love with your Father without beginning and your all-holy and life-giving Spirit, now and ever and forever. Amen.

HYMN

Let us sing a hymn of gladness,
Bringing God a song of praise,
For Saints Xenophon and Mary,
All the churches now shall raise
Thanks to God that fam'ly love
Burnished by baptismal grace
Caused these faithful ones to shine
In each circumstance and place.

Tell the story of this fam'ly
Who, 'midst strife and seeming loss,
Kept their focus on Christ Jesus,
Firmly clinging to His Cross.
Thanks to God that fam'ly love
Burnished by baptismal grace
Caused these faithful ones to shine
In each circumstance and place.

Glory let us give and blessing
To our God, the Three-in-One,
Father, Son, and Holy Spirit,
While eternal ages run!
Thanks to God that fam'ly love
Burnished by baptismal grace
Caused these faithful ones to shine
In each circumstance and place.

TUNE: *NACHE POVNYI HOLOS* / *WHAT A WONDROUS JOY*
TEXT: J. MICHAEL THOMPSON

A hymn for the Holy Venerable Martyrs Xenophon and Mary

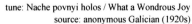

tune: Nache povnyi holos / What a Wondrous Joy
source: anonymous Galician (1920s)

1. Let us sing a hymn of glad - ness, Bring - ing
2. Tell the sto - ry of this fam - 'ly Who, 'midst
3. Glo - ry let us give and bles - sing To our

God a song of praise, For Saints Xe - no - phon and
strife and seem - ing loss, Kept their fo - cus on Christ
God, the Three - in - One, Fa - ther, Son, and Ho - ly

Ma - ry, All the church - es now shall raise
Je - sus, Firm - ly cling - ing to His Cross.
Spi - rit, While e - ter - nal a - ges run!

Thanks to God that fam - 'ly love Bur-nished by bap - tis - mal

grace Caused these faith - ful ones to shine In each

cir - cum - stance and place. place.

© 2013, J. Michael Thompson

SECTION III

HOLY MONASTICS

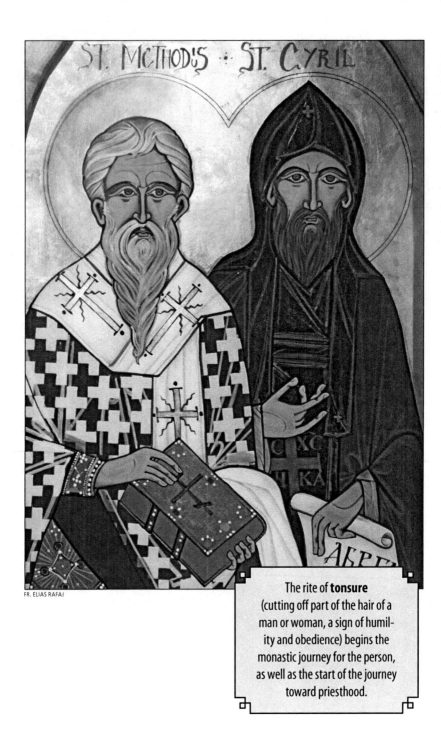

ST. METHODIS ÷ ST. CYRIL

FR. ELIAS RAFAJ

The rite of **tonsure** (cutting off part of the hair of a man or woman, a sign of humility and obedience) begins the monastic journey for the person, as well as the start of the journey toward priesthood.

VII

OUR HOLY FATHERS CYRIL AND METHODIUS, TEACHERS OF THE SLAVS AND EQUALS-TO-THE-APOSTLES

Feast Day: May 11

Many saints have influenced the Church, but few of them have left such a long-standing, culture-changing gift as that of these two Greek brothers we know today as St. Cyril and St. Methodius, "equals-to-the-Apostles" and "teachers of the Slavic people."

These two men were born in the Eastern Roman Empire to a family whose home was in Thessalonica. In this large family, Methodius was the oldest of seven brothers, and Constantine (he did not take the name of Cyril until he became a monk) was the youngest. Methodius was employed in the Byzantine army and became prefect of one of the Slavic areas conquered by the empire—most likely Bulgaria. It was there he first encountered and mastered the Slavic tongue. About ten years later, he was tonsured a monk. His brother, Constantine proved himself a brilliant student in several different fields of study.

The two brothers, known at the imperial court for their language skills, were given the task by the emperor of preaching the Christian faith to the Khazars, who lived in the Crimea (a peninsula of Ukraine). While preparing for their missionary journey, they visited the town of Korsun. There, the two came upon the relics of Pope St. Clement, who had been exiled to this area. At the same time, a request was forwarded to the emperor from Rostislav, prince of Moravia. He was experiencing pressure from the Holy Roman Empire and sought men from the Byzantine Empire who could come to his country to teach the Christian faith using the language of his people.

The emperor, aware this was a complicated political problem as well, had Constantine brought to him. He ordered Constantine to accept this new mission and told him to keep it a secret. The young man selected his older brother and five companions (Gorazd, Clement, Sava, Naum, and Angelyar) to accompany him on the journey. In preparation for this difficult task, he created a new script that permitted him to transcribe into the Slavonic language some of the books needed to celebrate the services of the Church. This massive work was accomplished in 893.

Thus prepared, the companions went to Moravia, where the prince and his people gladly received them. Immediately, they were able to teach the Moravian people the Good News in their own language. Missionary bishops, German in origin, celebrated the liturgy in the Latin tongue. These men were offended that the new missionaries were not celebrating in what they believed to be the holy languages used to label the cross of Jesus (Hebrew, Greek, and Latin). In response, Constantine said, "You only recognize three languages in which God may be glorified. But David sang, 'Praise the Lord, all nations, praise the Lord all peoples (Psalm 116:1).' And the Gospel of St. Matthew (28:18) says, 'Go and teach all nations....'" The German bishops had no adequate answer to this but instead complained to the pope in Rome, accusing the brothers of heresy.

Pope Adrian II called Constantine and Methodius to meet with him in Rome so this dispute might be settled. The brothers went there as requested, bringing with them the relics they had discovered of Pope St. Clement, third successor to the Apostle Peter as bishop of Rome. Having been informed that the delegation from Moravia was bringing the relics to Rome, the pope and his clergy processed to the city gates to solemnly receive them. Thus it was that Constantine and Methodius were received with the approval of the pope, who also ordered that the Slavonic Gospel brought by the brothers be placed in the church on the altar. The pope also gave these holy men permission to celebrate liturgical services in the Slavonic language.

While staying in Rome, Constantine became sick. Having received a warning from God that his illness would result in death, he requested and was given the monastic tonsure and the new name, Cyril. Living another fifty days after his reception of the monastic habit, he died at forty-two on the feast of St. Valentine the Roman martyr (February 14, 869). Among his last wishes, Cyril begged brother Methodius to return to Moravia to go on with the work of Christianizing the people. Methodius asked that the Holy Father return his brother's remains to Thessalonica for burial in his birthplace. The pope instead interred the Cyril's body in St. Clement's Church (which was also newly honored with the relics of the martyred pope that the two brothers had brought to Rome with them).

The pope consecrated Methodius as the missionary archbishop of Moravia and Pannonia and sent him to continue his evangelistic work. Upon arriving in Pannonia, Methodius taught the people there and celebrated the liturgy with the books in their language. This infuriated the German bishops, who arrested Methodius and took him to Swabia, where they kept him in prison for more than two years. Pope John VII ordered the captors to set Methodius free and return him to his archdiocese. Methodius returned and began again using the Slavonic language for preaching and liturgical services. The rulers of Bohemia were baptized due to the influence of Methodius and can be counted among his successes.

The German bishops began a third persecution of Methodius, this time accusing him of heresy because the Creed sung by the saint and his disciples was the original form, which did not include the phrase "and the Son." So once again, Methodius journeyed to Rome, where he was able to acquit himself of the charge of heresy. The pope accepted his defense and sent him back for a final time to the capital of Moravia, Velehrad.

It was there that Methodius spent the years left to him, continuing the translation work begun by Cyril. Knowing that death was approaching, he committed the work and the governing of the Moravian Church to his disciple, Gorazd. Methodius passed over from death to life on April 6, 885, and was buried in the cathedral church of Velehrad. Clergy gathered from far and wide for his funeral, and the service was sung in the three languages that the saint had preached in: Slavonic, Greek, and Latin.

SCRIPTURE

The eleven disciples went to Galilee, to the mountain to which Jesus had ordered them.

When they saw him, they worshiped, but they doubted.

Then Jesus approached and said to them, "All power in heaven and on earth has been given to me.

Go, therefore, and make disciples of all nations, baptizing them in the name of the Father, and of the Son, and of the holy Spirit,teaching them to observe all that I have commanded you.

And behold, I am with you always, until the end of the age."

MATTHEW 28:16–20

QUOTATION

We honor those priests who gave us the Light,
Who opened the fountain of theology for us
by translating the Holy Scriptures,
Thus starting a river from them that still runs today.
We glorify you, O Cyril and Methodius,
Who stand in heaven before the throne of the Lord on high
And who pray so fervently for all of us.

KONTAKION, TONE 3

REFLECTION

The saints show us what it means to follow Christ, even when things are difficult—or seemingly impossible. Cyril and Methodius persevered in their mission to bring the Good News of Jesus to the Slavic people in their own language, despite the persecution of those who should have known better. Are we following their example, "resisting the devil, steadfast in faith, knowing that our fellow believers throughout the world undergo the same sufferings" (see 1 Peter 5:9)?

PRAYER

O Christ, the giver of the new law of love, you have raised up in every age and in every land pastors and teachers faithful to your word, filled with zeal for bringing souls to you. We give you thanks for Saints Cyril and Methodius, the fathers of salvation for the Slavic peoples. Leaving home and family, they journeyed into new and unknown lands in order to share the Good News with those who had not yet had it proclaimed to them.

Gifted with skills of tongue and pen, they created an alphabet for the Slavonic language and used it to translate the holy Scriptures and the words of the divine liturgy into a new tongue. When faced with persecution from other Christians, they maintained their goal and traveled to Rome to have their mission and methods blessed by the Holy See. Despite the holy death of his brother, Cyril, your bishop Methodius returned to Moravia to continue the mission work until you at last called him to you in heaven. Keep us forever thankful for their work and raise up among us men and women like them who will carry your Gospel to every place on earth that needs to hear it. We give you glory, O Christ God, with the Father and the Holy Spirit, now and ever and forever. Amen.

HYMN

Our Church, in joyful chorus, now raises
From hearts and minds o'erflowing with love
Our hymns of thanks, full-throated with praises,
For our Apostles, guarding from above!
    For Cyril and Methodius, Lord,
    Your Church on earth will ev'ry praise afford!

Two brothers, called from home and comfort,
Brought Gospel joy to peoples untaught.
Through Word and Sacrament, they taught of
Christ, whose dear Blood their ransom had bought.
    For Cyril and Methodius, Lord,
    Your Church on earth will ev'ry praise afford!

Through strife and conflict, their work was ceaseless,
Teaching the Slavs in words all their own
Of God the Three-in-One, whose blessings
Made, with Christ's grace, their cornerstone.
    For Cyril and Methodius, Lord,
    Your Church on earth will ev'ry praise afford!

May we, their sons and daughters, e'er cherish
Strong in their faith, the Church of their dream,
That, growing daily in love and witness,
Our Church may thrive, in spite of plot and scheme.
    For Cyril and Methodius, Lord,
    Your Church on earth will ev'ry praise afford!

TUNE: *KOL' SLAVEN NASH* / *HOW GLORIOUS*

TEXT: J. MICHAEL THOMPSON

A hymn for our Holy Fathers Cyril and Methodius

tune: Kol' slaven nash / How Glorious
tune: D. Bortniansky (+1825)

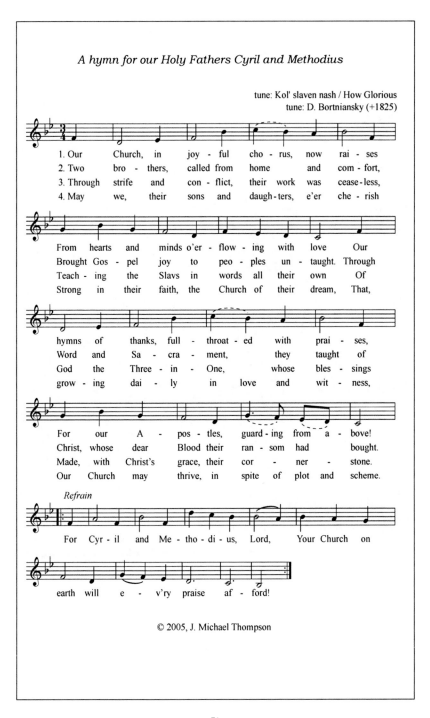

1. Our Church, in joy - ful cho - rus, now rai - ses
2. Two bro - thers, called from home and com - fort,
3. Through strife and con - flict, their work was cease - less,
4. May we, their sons and daugh - ters, e'er che - rish

From hearts and minds o'er - flow - ing with love Our
Brought Gos - pel joy to peo - ples un - taught. Through
Teach - ing the Slavs in words all their own Of
Strong in their faith, the Church of their dream, That,

hymns of thanks, full - throat - ed with prai - ses,
Word and Sa - cra - ment, they taught of
God the Three - in - One, whose bles - sings
grow - ing dai - ly in love and wit - ness,

For our A - pos - tles, guard - ing from a - bove!
Christ, whose dear Blood their ran - som had bought.
Made, with Christ's grace, their cor - ner - stone.
Our Church may thrive, in spite of plot and scheme.

Refrain

For Cyr - il and Me - tho - di - us, Lord, Your Church on

earth will e - v'ry praise af - ford!

© 2005, J. Michael Thompson

71

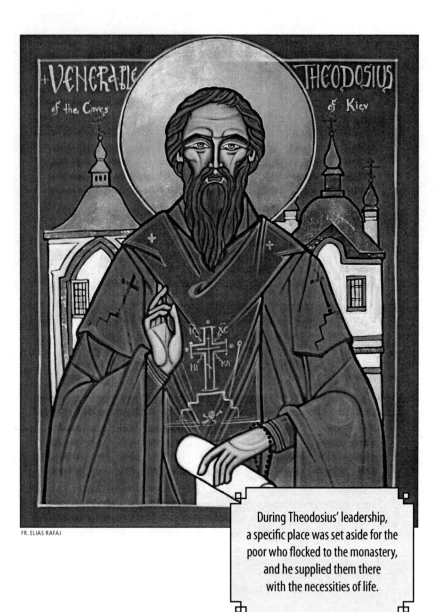

+ VENERABLE · THEODOSIUS
of the Caves · of Kiev

IC XC
NI KA

FR. ELIAS RAFAJ

During Theodosius' leadership,
a specific place was set aside for the
poor who flocked to the monastery,
and he supplied them there
with the necessities of life.

VIII

OUR VENERABLE FATHER THEODOSIUS OF THE MONASTERY OF THE CAVES IN KIEV

Feast Day: May 3

Recognized by all as the co-father of monasticism in Kievan Rus', Theodosius (1009–1074) was born at Vasilevo, located near Kiev. Even as a young child, he was drawn to the life of the desert fathers and emulated them even while living in the home of his parents. Unlike most of his age group, he preferred attending services in the church to playing with others. His strongest wish was to undertake learning to read and then to study the Scriptures, in particular the Psalms. His parents gave permission for this, and all the neighbors were astounded at his ability both to read and to understand the books he loved.

A major change for Theodosius came in his fourteenth year, at the death of his father. The youth remained in the custody and under the tutelage of his mother, whose love for her son was enmeshed with her desire that he remain with her in his native village. When he reached twenty-four, Theodosius left home without telling anyone where he was going. He journeyed to Kiev and sought the blessing of the hegumen (the head) of the Monastery of the Caves, St. Anthony. Anthony received him and tonsured him. He remained there for four years, when his mother discovered him. She pleaded with him to return to their village, but Theodosius managed to convince her to move to Kiev. She was received as a nun in the women's monastery of St. Nicholas.

In the monastery, the young monk was known among the brethren for his commitment to the community's chores. Often he did both his own work and that of some of his fellow monks, grinding grain and moving flour, chopping wood and carrying water for his brothers. He disciplined his body, ignoring the cold and the insects that tormented him. While he worked with his hands, he chanted the Psalter, which he knew by heart. His community found that Theodosius was the first to be in the church for services and remained in his stall until the service was completely finished. One of the things remarked about him was the intensity with which he attended to the reading of holy Scripture. In obedience to the hegumen, he was ordained to the holy priesthood in 1054. Upon the death of the hegumen, Theodosius was elected to be his successor.

Theodosius' reputation as a holy and wise man brought new vocations to the monastery. Because of this, a new church and additional housing were added to the Monastery of the Caves. It was Theodosius who introduced the Rule from the Studion monastery in Constantinople to the monks of Kievan Rus', thus bringing the cenobitic form of life to his land. One of his great projects was to improve the care for those who had no resources whatsoever. During Theodosius' hegumenate, a specific place was set aside for the poor who flocked to the monastery, and he supplied them there with the necessities of life. The monk was particularly concerned for the destitute.

When he became aware that his death was imminent, he prepared his brethren for his departure and passed over to the Lord on May 3, 1074. His monks buried him in the cave that had been dug by the saint's own hands, where he had spent time alone during the liturgical times of strict fasting.

SCRIPTURE

[But] whatever gains I had, these I have come to consider a loss because of Christ.

More than that, I even consider everything as a loss because of the supreme good of knowing Christ Jesus my Lord. For his sake I have accepted the loss of all things and I consider them so much rubbish, that I may gain Christ

and be found in him, not having any righteousness of my own based on the law but that which comes through faith in Christ, the righteousness from God, depending on faith

to know him and the power of his resurrection and [the] sharing of his sufferings by being conformed to his death, if somehow I may attain the resurrection from the dead.

PHILIPPIANS 3:7–11

QUOTATION

Loving the monastic life from your youth, you climbed the summit of virtue.

Achieving your goal, you took up life in a cave.

Perfecting your life by fasting, you became like an angel.

You have enlightened all the Slav lands like a star.

O father Theodosius, intercede with Christ our God to save our souls.

TROPARION, TONE 8

REFLECTION

Even living as a recluse, St. Theodosius was a witness to the incredible power of Jesus Christ to save and transform lives. Instead of being angry with people who disturbed his desire for solitude with Christ, he served the poor and the needy (both temporally and spiritually). Do we balance the need for an interior life with the need to serve Christ in others?

PRAYER

O Christ God, as you called your priest Samuel when he was only a child to hear you and to serve you, so you inspired the holy Theodosius. In his youth, he yearned to serve you as a monk, so you filled his heart and mind with the study of your holy word and the ways of the fathers and mothers before him.

Leaving home and family, he found you and served you in his brethren who followed after him. He cared for the poor and needy and never turned away anyone who sought a listening ear. You made him a beloved mentor for all of the people of Rus', and we thank you for his constancy in your service. Create in us, O Lord, hearts that are open to your call and that lead us into lives of service for your people in need. Glory to you, O Christ our God, together with your Father without beginning and your all-holy and life-giving Spirit, now and ever and forever. Amen.

HYMN

From earliest youth you heard the call of the Lord,
Leaving home and family to serve with one accord.
Theodosius, father of monastic ways,
Pray to Christ that we serve Him all our days.

You sought the counsel of the wise Anthony,
Turning from all earthly cares to live life full and free.
Theodosius, father of monastic ways,
Pray to Christ that we serve Him all our days.

Your meekness and ascetic life awed your peers,
Calling them to leave the world and cast aside all fears.
Theodosius, father of monastic ways,
Pray to Christ that we serve Him all our days.

So teach us, too, to seek Christ's will in our life,
Biding faithful to His Word despite all stress and strife.
Theodosius, father of monastic ways,
Pray to Christ that we serve Him all our days.

TUNE: *O Marija Mati Bozha / O Mary, Mother of Our God*

TEXT: J. MICHAEL THOMPSON

A hymn for our Venerable Father Theodosius of the Caves

tune: O Marija Mati Boža / O Mary, Mother of Our God
source: Užhorod "Pisennik" (1913)

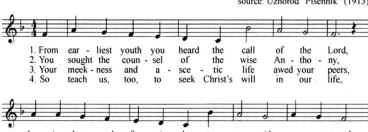

1. From ear - liest youth you heard the call of the Lord,
2. You sought the coun - sel of the wise An - tho - ny,
3. Your meek - ness and a - sce - tic life awed your peers,
4. So teach us, too, to seek Christ's will in our life,

Leav - ing home and fam - i - ly to serve with one ac - cord.
Turn - ing from all earth - ly cares to live life full and free.
Cal - ling them to leave the world and cast a - side all fears.
Bid - ing faith - ful to His Word de - spite all stress and strife.

Refrain

The - o - do - si - us, fa - ther of mo - nas - tic ways,

Pray to Christ that we serve Him all our days.

© 2013, J. Michael Thompson

SAINT of DAVID
Thessalonica

You made a tree your dwelling O David from where you soared to Heaven

FR. ELIAS RAFAJ

Moved by examples of Old Testament patriarchs and prophets, David lived in an almond tree for three years, then resumed life in a monastery.

IX

OUR VENERABLE
FATHER DAVID
OF THESSALONICA

Feast Day: June 26

At one time, it was common to say of a person who behaved oddly that he was "out of his tree." In the case of St. David of Thessalonica, his particular response to his vocation instead was to climb into a tree, where he spent three years totally exposed to the extremes of weather.

David was originally from Mesopotamia, and no one is quite certain what brought him from the Middle East to the city of Thessalonica in Greece. As a young man, he was granted entrance to the Monastery of Saints Theodore and Mecurius, which was situated near the wall of the city. Moved by the examples of the patriarchs and prophets of the Old Testament, David climbed high into the branches of an almond tree next to the church of his monastery, and there he remained for the next three years. At the end of that three-year period, an angel told David that he should climb down from the tree and resume life in the monastery. The saint did so, and—in the presence of the bishop of Thessalonica—entered into the cell where he dwelt for the rest of his life.

The reputation of David's ascetic life spread throughout the region, and many people came to him for advice about their spiritual lives. He attended to them from his cell. However, his solitude was interrupted when his new bishop asked him to journey to Constantinople to plead with the emperor over an important need of the city of Thessalonica. Obediently he went off to the capital city, where he was received with respect by its citizens. The empress asked him to stay in the palace, where the emperor was to meet with him. And in the presence of the entire Senate, the Emperor Justinian met with him. At that time, the saint took a burning coal into his bare hand, sprinkled incense on the coal, and proceeded to honor the emperor with it, all without being harmed. He then made his petition to the emperor on behalf of the city of Thessalonica. The emperor granted the city's request, and David boarded a ship to return home.

On the journey home, he became aware that the Lord was about to call him. He died in the city of Emvolos, where his last wishes were to have his body returned to his own monastery. His desire was granted, and so his body was buried at the Monastery of Saints Theodore and Mecurius. After the Fourth Crusade (1204), crusaders took his relics from Thessalonica and moved them to Pavia in Italy. Years later, they were moved again to the city of Milan. Finally, in 1978, at the request of the bishop of Thessalonica, the relics were returned to that city, where they were enshrined in the Basilica of St. Demetrius the Great-Martyr. September 16 is kept as the feast of the translation of his relics.

SCRIPTURE

If then you were raised with Christ, seek what is above, where Christ is seated at the right hand of God.

Think of what is above, not of what is on earth.

For you have died, and your life is hidden with Christ in God.

When Christ your life appears, then you too will appear with him in glory.

Put to death, then, the parts of you that are earthly: immorality, impurity, passion, evil desire, and the greed that is idolatry.

Because of these the wrath of God is coming [upon the disobedient].

By these you too once conducted yourselves, when you lived in that way.

But now you must put them all away: anger, fury, malice, slander, and obscene language out of your mouths.

Stop lying to one another, since you have taken off the old self with its practices

and have put on the new self, which is being renewed, for knowledge, in the image of its creator.

Here there is not Greek and Jew, circumcision and uncircumcision, barbarian, Scythian, slave, free; but Christ is all and in all.

Colossians 3:1–11

QUOTATION

You were like a perpetually blooming orchard,

Continually bearing the fruits of good works.

You were like a bird with a beautiful song, O David.

Within your heart, you found the tree of life in the Lord,

Even more surely than on the fields of paradise.

You tended it carefully and nourished it with grace.

Always pray for us, O blessed David!

KONTAKION, TONE 2

REFLECTION

We are often guilty of judging a person by what we see, without knowing what is truly going on in a person's heart. How a person dresses, how he or she behaves—these criteria often cause us to make a snap judgment that keeps us from seeing what sort of person is behind the clothing or social status. The life of St. David and his unusual dwelling in a tree, if viewed separately from the teaching and the good deeds of his life, can distract us from his lifelong intention, which was to give glory to God and to build up God's holy people, the Church. Today is a good time to see how discerning we really are by checking out whether our judgment is superficial, or instead, does it regard matters that extend into eternity?

PRAYER

All-merciful Christ our God, you called the publican Zacchaeus down from a tree so that he might be your host and thus brought him to salvation. We give you thanks on this day for our Venerable Father David of Thessalonica, whom you called to take his abode in a tree, that he might seek you and you alone. Within branches of the almond tree, he came to a knowledge of you and, by doing so, emptied himself of all things that separate humankind from union with you.

Lord God, your glory was made manifest through your servant David of Thessalonica, as you gave him wisdom and the ability to work wonders for your name's sake both in the Church and in the world around him. Teach us to surrender to your holy will in our lives and to glorify you, not only with our words, but in our deeds as well. We join our voices with your servant David of Thessalonica and with all the saints and angels, who give you glory, O Christ, and to your Father and to the Holy Spirit, now and ever and forever. Amen.

HYMN

Jesus, Lord, we sing Your glory,
Joy of monks, their Truth and Life!
In the midst of toil and struggle,
You are refuge from earth's strife.
> For Your saints, Lord, we sing!
> May our song for them take wing!
> All our praise, O Lord, we bring!

Good Saint David built a shelter
In a leafy almond tree,
Where in solitude and silence
He from passions was made free.
> For Your saints, Lord, we sing!
> May our song for them take wing!
> All our praise, O Lord, we bring!

Once when greeting earthly ruler,
He took live coal in his hand,
Censed the Emperor, who bowed down
Awed to see what God had planned.
> For Your saints, Lord, we sing!
> May our song for them take wing!
> All our praise, O Lord, we bring!

Father, Son, and Holy Spirit,
Holy God both Three and One,
Let us follow good Saint David,
That Your will be ever done!
> For Your saints, Lord, we sing!
> May our song for them take wing!
> All our praise, O Lord, we bring!

TUNE: *VESELISJA* / *REJOICE, O PUREST MOTHER*
TEXT: J. MICHAEL THOMPSON

A hymn for our Venerable Father David of Thessalonica

tune: Veselisja / Rejoice, O Purest Mother
source: Užhorod "Pisennik" (1913)

1. Je - sus, Lord, we sing Your glo - ry, Joy of monks, their Truth and Life!
2. Good Saint Da - vid built a shel - ter In a lea - fy al - mond tree,
3. Once when greet - ing earth - ly ru - ler, He took live coal in his hand,
4. Fa - ther, Son, and Ho - ly Spi - rit, Ho - ly God both Three and One,

In the midst of toil and strug - gle, You are re - fuge from earth's strife.
Where in so - li - tude and si - lence He from pas - sions was made free.
Censed the Em - pe - ror, who bowed down Awed to see what God had planned.
Let us fol - low good Saint Da - vid, that Your will be e - ver done!

Refrain

For Your saints, Lord, we sing! May our song for them take wing!

All our praise, O Lord, we bring!

© 2006, J. Michael Thompson

SAINT MAXIMOS THE CON-FESSOR

Monothelitism argues that Jesus has two natures but only one will. This is **false** because Christianity professes that Jesus has two wills: human and divine.

Monophysitism argues that Jesus has only one nature. This is also **false** because Christianity teaches that Jesus' nature is both human and divine.

FR. ELIAS RAFAJ

X

OUR VENERABLE FATHER MAXIMUS THE CONFESSOR

Feast Day: January 21

What is one to do when the prevailing spirit of the era seems to be contrary to the spirit of the Gospel? Is the better idea to "flee the world" and keep one's soul safe? Or should one stay and fight for the truth? The life of Maximus the Confessor illumines for us the pros and cons of both responses.

Maximus was born in or around the year 580 in the city of Constantinople. His parents were known to be both devout and orthodox in their Christian faith. Because of them, Maximus was given an education that few others received, permitting him to advance in the studies of rhetoric, philosophy, and grammar. When he completed his studies, he was taken into the imperial bureaucracy and assigned the position of first secretary (asekretis), which placed him as the chief counselor to the Emperor Heraclius (610–641). The emperor was much taken with the young man's intelligence and his pious way of life.

However, it soon became apparent to Maximus that much of the imperial court, including the emperor, had been infected with the Monothelite heresy. Once he became aware of this, Maximus turned in his resignation from all courtly responsibilities, proceeding to the Chrysopolis monastery, where he was tonsured and received as a monk. Maximus' learning and humility won the respect of his new community, and they elected him to be hegumen of the monastery after only a short time there. Despite this promotion, he lived as an ordinary member of the monastery. Maximus journeyed to Jerusalem, to Africa, and then finally to Rome. At the Lateran Council of 549, the Church condemned the heresies of Monotheletism and Monophysitism. Maximus was present at the council.

Upon his return to Constantinople after the council, Maximus was imprisoned for the crime of treason by the emperor. For their crime, the saint and two of his disciples each had their tongues removed and their right hands cut off. After these tortures, they were then sent into exile in Skhemaris on the Black Sea. The journey was exceedingly harsh, and the men suffered much along the way. Maximus was called to the Lord on August 13, 662. His feast is kept in the Byzantine Churches on January 21.

SCRIPTURE

What was from the beginning,

what we have heard,

what we have seen with our eyes,

what we looked upon

and touched with our hands

concerns the Word of life—

for the life was made visible;

we have seen it and testify to it

and proclaim to you the eternal life

that was with the Father and was made visible to us—

what we have seen and heard

we proclaim now to you,

so that you too may have fellowship with us;

for our fellowship is with the Father

and with his Son, Jesus Christ.

We are writing this so that our joy may be complete.

Now this is the message that we have heard from him and proclaim to you: God is light, and in him there is no darkness at all.

If we say, "We have fellowship with him," while we continue to walk in darkness, we lie and do not act in truth.

But if we walk in the light as he is in the light, then we have fellowship with one another, and the blood of his Son Jesus cleanses us from all sin.

If we say, "We are without sin," we deceive ourselves, and the truth is not in us.

If we acknowledge our sins, he is faithful and just and will forgive our sins and cleanse us from every wrongdoing.

1 John 1:1–9

QUOTATION

Let us, O faithful, honor with worthy hymns the great Maximus,

So highly devoted to the Holy Trinity.

He preached faith in God with great courage,

And glorified Christ in His two natures,
two wills, and two operations.

Therefore, let us cry out:

Rejoice, O preacher of the true faith!

KONTAKION, TONE 8

REFLECTION

One of the amazing things about the saints of the Christian East is their connection to the dogmatic teachings of the faith, which is reflected not only in their lives and in their writings but also in the hymns of the services sung in their honor. Because of this liturgical practice, there is no disconnection between the ancient heresies and the life of the contemporary Christian. For me, then, when I read words such as "Monothelite," do I simply skip over them or do I take the time to see how this heresy not only affected the time of St. Maximus but is also found in my own time?

PRAYER

O Christ, truly God and truly man, we give you praise and worship for your wonderful Incarnation. Eternally begotten of God the Father, you took flesh of the all-pure and ever-virgin Mary and became one of us, like us in all things except for sin. We thank you for the work of theologians such as our holy Father Maximus the Confessor, who defended the union of your two natures, each with its own will. Through his faithfulness to the Church's teaching about you, O Lord, he was subjected to horrible torture and mutilation; yet, in spite of all, he refused to deny your truth.

Give us, O Christ, the same firm commitment to you, the Way, the Truth, and the Life, that we may be willing to give up everything rather than to betray you. You are the Light of your people, and we give glory to you and to your Father who had no beginning, and to your all-holy and life-giving Spirit, now and ever and forever. Amen.

HYMN

In Christ, who is both God and human,
Having two wills and energies,
The love of God is shown in fullness,
Love that creates and love that frees.
> For Maximus, our ven'rable father,
> On this glad day, our hymns of thanks we raise!

In Maximus, the abbot and teacher,
Your Church is led in ways of truth,
And in his fearful exile and passion,
He shepherds all, both aged and youth.
> For Maximus, our ven'rable father,
> On this glad day, our hymns of thanks we raise!

His writings taught of Christ our Savior;
His actions proved he knew his Lord.
In loss of tongue and right hand to torture,
He caused his Christ to be adored!
> For Maximus, our ven'rable father,
> On this glad day, our hymns of thanks we raise!

O Father, Son, and Holy Spirit,
Trinity blest: we sing your praise!
For Maximus and all your martyrs,
We will give thanks through all our days!
> For Maximus, our ven'rable father,
> On this glad day, our hymns of thanks we raise!

TUNE: *Kol' slaven nash* / *How Glorious Is Our God*
TEXT: J. MICHAEL THOMPSON

A hymn for our Venerable Father Maximus the Confessor

tune: Kol' slaven nash / How Glorious Is Our God
tune: D. Bortniansky (+1825)

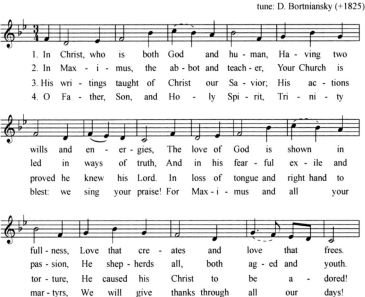

1. In Christ, who is both God and hu - man, Ha - ving two
2. In Max - i - mus, the ab - bot and teach - er, Your Church is
3. His wri - tings taught of Christ our Sa - vior; His ac - tions
4. O Fa - ther, Son, and Ho - ly Spi - rit, Tri - ni - ty

wills and en - er - gies, The love of God is shown in
led in ways of truth, And in his fear - ful ex - ile and
proved he knew his Lord. In loss of tongue and right hand to
blest: we sing your praise! For Max - i - mus and all your

full - ness, Love that cre - ates and love that frees.
pas - sion, He shep - herds all, both ag - ed and youth.
tor - ture, He caused his Christ to be a - dored!
mar - tyrs, We will give thanks through all our days!

Refrain

For Max - i - mus, our ven - 'ra - ble fa - ther, On this glad

day, our hymns of thanks we raise!

© 2005, J. Michael Thompson

SECTION IV

SAINTS ON BOTH EASTERN
AND WESTERN CALENDARS

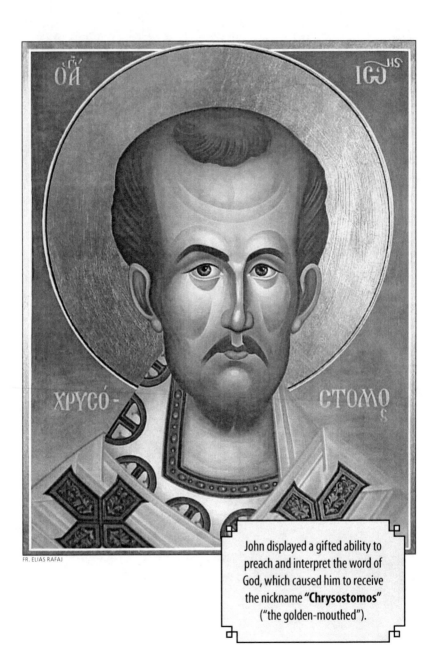

ὉΆ   ΙϹͩ

ΧΡΥϹΌ-   ϹΤΟΜΟϹ

FR. ELIAS RAFAJ

John displayed a gifted ability to preach and interpret the word of God, which caused him to receive the nickname **"Chrysostomos"** ("the golden-mouthed").

XI

OUR HOLY FATHER
JOHN CHRYSOSTOM,
ARCHBISHOP OF CONSTANTINOPLE

Feast Day: November 13

Why are we greatly loved by some and intensely despised by others? A thorough examination of the life of St. John Chrysostom may help us understand this paradox.

Born into a military family in the city of Antioch in the year 347, John's intelligence was obvious from an early age. He was privileged to learn from some of the finest professors of both rhetoric and philosophy. This learning, however, left him feeling empty inside. In his youth, the saintly Meletius, who was then the bishop of Antioch, mentored John. The bishop had great affection for the young man and took it upon himself to direct him in the knowledge and love of the Lord, baptizing the saint in the year 367. Three years after his baptism, the bishop ordained John as a reader. When Emperor Valens exiled Bishop Meletius in the year 372, John and his fellow student Theodore of Mopsuestia were impelled to continue learning. The priests Flavian and Diodorus of Tarsus directed these young men. Diodorus, more than any of his other professors, exerted particular influence on John.

Upon the death of his mother, John was accepted into a monastery. He was later to call monasticism the "true philosophy." Before long, both

John and his dear friend Basil were being sought after to become bishops. Both were completely opposed to this, so they opted instead to go into the desert. This escape worked for John, but in secret he worked for the ordination of Basil to the episcopacy.

John spent two years in isolation in the caves of the desert without speaking to anyone. He seriously damaged his health by doing so and returned to Antioch to try to recuperate. While he was being nursed back to health, John was ordained to the diaconate by his mentor, Meletius, in 381. Five years later, Bishop Flavian ordained John to the priesthood for the Church of Antioch. In those years, John displayed a gifted ability to preach and interpret the word of God, which caused him to receive the nickname "Chrysostomos" (that is, "the golden-mouthed"). For the next twelve years John's preaching was heard at least twice weekly, with the faithful flocking to hear him.

In 397, following the death of Nectarius, the archbishop of Constantinople, John was called from Antioch to the capital of the empire and found himself elected as the next archbishop. Now John found considerably less time to preach than he previously had. The administration of the diocese took an immense amount of his time. He began his work there with a concern dear to his heart, that is, the local priesthood and its growth in holiness. While this was not a universally popular concept, it was obvious that John was, himself, living exactly as he taught. His concern for the poor, the sick, and pilgrims diverted much of the funds available to him into the setting up of hospitals and pilgrims' inns. His lifestyle was ascetic, and he fasted strictly, often turning down dinner invitations because his stomach was not up to the rich meals often served in the capital.

His blunt speech was soon directed against the immorality of many of his sons and daughters, most explicitly those who were part of the court of the emperor and his wife. Eventually John came into direct conflict with Empress Eudoxia, who organized clerics who had been disciplined by John for transgressing the canons. These clerics set up a kangaroo court, which arranged the exile of the archbishop. As he was ready to leave the city, an earthquake occurred, which frightened the empress so much she asked the emperor to rescind the decree of exile. But after only two months, the empress once again organized a council of bishops opposed to John. He was again exiled, and this time the long journey killed him. Having been informed by a vision of the day of his death, he received the holy mysteries (the Eucharist as viaticum) and then was taken to the Lord on the feast of the Universal Exaltation of the Precious and Life-Giving Cross (September 14), 407. His last words have come down in history to us: "Glory to God for all things!"

Since he died on a major feast of the Lord, the Byzantine Church changed the feast day of the saint to November 13.

QUOTATION

The grace shining forth from your mouth like a torch

Has enlightened the universe;

It has stored up in the world the treasure of disdain for wealth.

It has shown us the heights of Humility.

Instruct us by your words, John Chrysostom our father,

And intercede with the Word, Christ God, to save our souls.

TROPARION, TONE 8

SCRIPTURE

I, then, a prisoner for the Lord, urge you to live in a manner worthy of the call you have received,

with all humility and gentleness, with patience, bearing with one another through love,

striving to preserve the unity of the spirit through the bond of peace:

one body and one Spirit, as you were also called to the one hope of your call; one Lord, one faith, one baptism; one God and Father of all, who is over all and through all and in all.

But grace was given to each of us according to the measure of Christ's gift.

Therefore, it says: "He ascended on high and took prisoners captive; he gave gifts to men."

What does "he ascended" mean except that he also descended into the lower [regions] of the earth?

The one who descended is also the one who ascended far above all the heavens, that he might fill all things.

And he gave some as apostles, others as prophets, others as evangelists, others as pastors and teachers, to equip the holy ones for the work of ministry, for building up the body of Christ,

until we all attain to the unity of faith and knowledge of the Son of God, to mature manhood, to the extent of the full stature of Christ,

so that we may no longer be infants, tossed by waves and swept along by every wind of teaching arising from human trickery, from their cunning in the interests of deceitful scheming.

Rather, living the truth in love, we should grow in every way into him who is the head, Christ,

from whom the whole body, joined and held together by every supporting ligament, with the proper functioning of each part, brings about the body's growth and builds itself up in love.

EPHESIANS 4:1–16

REFLECTION

St. John Chrysostom has been called a second Apostle Paul, with his incredible gifts of preaching and teaching. He was also similar to the great apostle in his rather irascible nature, which did not suffer fools gladly. However, the poor and the outcast found in John a ready ear and an open hand. In the words of the poet Phyllis McGinley (speaking of yet another irascible saint), "But he raised men's minds with a Christian leaven. It takes all kinds to make a heaven." Do we ask for the grace to work beyond our natural limitations?

PRAYER

O Christ, living Word of the Father, we give you thanks for the gifts of preaching and teaching that you have bestowed on your servant, the Archbishop John. So united was he to your truth that the Church has named him "the golden-mouthed." We approach your heavenly throne with the words of his divine liturgy, where we are taught to lay aside each earthly care so we might receive you, the king of all.

John's fearless preaching of your Gospel was accompanied by intense love for the poor and the needy, both of which often provoked envy and anger among those who loved themselves more than you. For this he suffered exile and imprisonment, which he accepted with humility as though from your hand. Teach us through his words and actions to love only you and to follow you no matter how difficult the path until we come to join you with him and all the white-robed army without number around your throne, where you live and reign with the Father and the Holy Spirit, God forever and ever. Amen.

HYMN

For Chrysostom, the golden-tongued,
We give You praise, O Lord;
Through ministry of spoken word
He made Your Name adored.
As bishop, John has fed Your flock,
Not fleeing as hired hand;
And through derision, exile, loss,
Come at Your side to stand.

His gift of preaching caused the Word
To be a living thing,
And through his awesome gift of words
He bade his people sing.
He loved the poor and needy, Lord;
He pastored well your sheep;
Though exiled for his obstinance,
Your Church he safe did keep.

O Father, Son, and Spirit blest,
O Godhead, one-in-three,
May songs of praise be now addressed
From those Your grace set free.
With holy father Chrysostom
And saints' and angels' throng,
We set aside all earthly cares
To praise in mystic song.

TUNE: *POD TVOJ POKROV* / *WE HASTEN TO YOUR PATRONAGE*

TEXT: J. MICHAEL THOMPSON

A hymn for our Holy Father John Chrysostom

tune: Pod tvoj pokrov / We Hasten to Your Patronage
source: Užhorod "Pisennik" (1913)

1. For Chry - so - stom, the gol - den - tongued, We
2. His gift of preach - ing caused the Word To
3. O Fa - ther, Son, and Spi - rit blest, O

give You praise, O Lord; Through min - i - stry of
be a liv - ing thing, And through his awe - some
God - head, one - in - three, May songs of praise be

spo - ken word He made Your Name a - dored. As
gift of words He bade his peo - ple sing. He
now ad - dressed From those Your grace set free. With

bi - shop, John has fed Your flock, Not flee - ing
loved the poor and need - y, Lord; He pas - tored
ho - ly fa - ther Chry - so - stom And saints' and

as hired hand; And through de - ri - sion,
well your sheep; Though ex - iled for his
an - gels' throng, We set a - side all

ex - ile, loss, Come at Your side to stand.
ob - sti - nance, Your Church he safe did keep.
earth - ly cares To praise in mys - tic song.

© 2005, J. Michael Thompson

FR. ELIAS RAFAJ

St. John, living in a **Muslim** world, grew up respecting the beliefs of others while remaining centered in **Christianity**.

XII

OUR VENERABLE FATHER JOHN OF DAMASCUS

Feast Day: December 4

Living as we do in a multicultural world, it is good to examine the life of a saint who lived in that same sort of world and made huge contributions to the Church.

John, the son of Sergius Mansur, was born in the city of Damascus around the year 680. Syria had been conquered by the Muslims and was no longer part of the Byzantine Empire. Christians were often in positions of great public authority. In fact, John's father was one of the treasurers in the caliph's court. Upon the death of his father, the young John became a civil servant, following in his father's footsteps. His acumen led the caliph to appoint him to the position of city prefect.

The Eastern Church was going through some very rough times. A movement called "iconoclasm" (that is, the rejection or destruction of icons) threatened the unity of the Church in the capital of the Byzantine Empire (Constantinople). This movement forbade the use of images of any sort in Christian worship as they were denounced as being contrary to the commandment: "You shall not make for yourself an idol...you shall not bow down before them or serve them" (Exodus 20:3–5). Thus, iconoclasts forcibly removed icons of our Lord, the *Theotokos*, and the saints from churches.

Leo III the Isaurian (717–741), was a powerful supporter of this heresy. Writing from Damascus, John defended the use of icons in Christian worship by stating that, because the Word of God became flesh in Jesus Christ, depicting his image was, in fact, a defense of the Incarnation. The saint put forth his thoughts on the matter in a treatise called *Against Those Who Revile the Holy Icons*. St. John wrote the *Three Treatises on the Divine Images*, which was essentially the same defense against the iconoclasts emphasized three separate times.

This gave those who defended the use of icons in worship (called "iconodules" from the Greek word for the "venerators of icons") a theological basis to oppose the emperor's policies. These writings angered the emperor, but since John was not a resident of the Byzantine Empire, he was not vulnerable to arrest or death by Byzantine authority. This required the emperor to engage in an oblique attack. He did so by forging a letter purportedly by John, in which "John" offered to help the Byzantine emperor arrange for a treasonous betrayal of the city of Damascus to the troops. The false letter indicated that John was going to help deliver the Syrian capital of Damascus into Byzantine hands.

So Emperor Leo III sent this forgery to the caliph of Damascus, who then ordered that John should lose his post as prefect and suffer by having his treasonous right hand chopped off. John was then dragged in chains throughout the city of Damascus. Later that day, the guards returned to John the hand that had been cut off. Oral history records John taking the hand, placing it against his wrist, and seeking the intercession of the *Theotokos* and ever-virgin Mary so he might continue his writing in service to the Church. John fell asleep before her icon and while asleep he was told by the Blessed Virgin that his healing was granted and that John could work without stopping. When John arose, he saw that his hand had been reattached, with only a small scar to bear witness to the wonder achieved for him.

As a result of this healing, John hastened to take the wealth that he had inherited, distributing it to the poor of the city. He then left Damascus and journeyed to the holy city of Jerusalem in the company of Cosmas, his stepbrother. Both went to the monastery of Mar Saba and were tonsured as novices in the monastic community. John's fame had preceded him to the monastery, and it proved difficult for him to find a spiritual father who was not intimidated by John's social status and his intellectual achievements. There was one in the community who was skilled in training men to become humble and obedient monks. This monk told John he was to take no action of his own accord. In other words, he was to submit his whole will to the guidance of the spiritual father.

When death unexpectedly took one of the brethren, the monk's brother asked John to write a hymn to be used at the funeral. John put the monk off but eventually complied. His composition, a series of hymns in all eight of the Byzantine tones, is used to this day in the Byzantine funeral service. Upon hearing of this act of willful disobedience, John's spiritual father cut him off from counsel and refused to forgive him. Other members of the community interceded for him, imploring the father to give John a severe penance. The saint agreed to this and fulfilled it joyfully.

The *Theotokos* herself told the spiritual father that John must be permitted to write again in the service of the Church. John's skill at writing both theological treatises and liturgical hymnody came to the attention of the patriarch of Jerusalem. He summoned John to the holy city where he was made a presbyter and given the office of public preacher.

This public life was not a good match for John, however, and he was permitted to return to the Mar Saba monastery, where he continued his vocation of writing. After his return from Jerusalem, his only journey was to attend the Church council held to condemn the Iconoclast heresy, held in 754 in the city of Constantinople. While there, the emperor had him arrested and tortured. John endured this and was eventually released to return to his monastery. He fell asleep in the Lord in 780.

SCRIPTURE

For this reason, I remind you to stir into flame the gift of God that you have through the imposition of my hands.

For God did not give us a spirit of cowardice but rather of power and love and self-control.

So do not be ashamed of your testimony to our Lord, nor of me, a prisoner for his sake; but bear your share of hardship for the gospel with the strength that comes from God.

He saved us and called us to a holy life, not according to our works but according to his own design and the grace bestowed on us in Christ Jesus before time began,

but now made manifest through the appearance of our savior Christ Jesus, who destroyed death and brought life and immortality to light through the gospel.

2 TIMOTHY 1:6–10

QUOTATION

Let us praise John the hymnographer with song.

He is an effective preacher and a teacher for the Church.

Behind the armor of the Cross, he exposed the lies of heresy,

And standing before God, he obtains the remission of sins for us.

KONTAKION, TONE 4

REFLECTION

We live in a world that is multicultural and multireligious. It is a challenge to do so—to be both respectful of the beliefs of others and still centered in the truth of the Christian faith. St. John, living in a Muslim world, grew up balancing these two realities and did so without ever sacrificing the Gospel of Jesus Christ. How are we living with this balance in our lives?

PRAYER

O Christ, your resurrection has brought all creation to new life! We thank you for the words of St. John of Damascus, whose hymns are sung week by week in your Church, giving glory to your victory over sin and death. His defense of the holy icons is, in fact, a defense of your condescension in taking on our human nature through the *Theotokos* and ever-virgin Mary. His systematic teaching of the Orthodox and Catholic faith helped codify the teachings of the fathers who went before him.

Living a life of great humility, he was opened to your divine majesty, of which he sang in deathless and beautiful words. Help us to sing these hymns to you, O Lord, with the same singleness of heart that marked John's whole life. For you are a God of victory over death, O Christ, and we give you glory with your Father and the Holy Spirit, now and ever and forever. Amen.

HYMN

O Love of God, who for our sake
Our nature and our flesh did take,
We give You highest praise today;
For saintly John our thanks we pay.

Defender of the Faith was he,
Called preacher, writer, sage to be
Summation of the Fathers' lore,
That we be faithful, as before.

Proclaimer of the icon's role
To testify the awesome goal
That Christ, true God, became true man,
Fulfilling thus His saving plan.

A singer of the Trinity
Was John, whose hymns will ever be
A bedrock of the Church's song,
Where truth and beauty fight the wrong.

To You, O Father, source and end,
To You, O Christ, both Lord and friend,
To You, O Spirit, grace's spring,
O Three-in-One, our praise we bring.

TUNE: *DAMASCUS*
TEXT: J. MICHAEL THOMPSON

A hymn for our Venerable Father John of Damascus

tune: Damascus
author: J. Michael Thompson (2013)

1. O Love of God, who for our sake Our na - ture and our
2. De- fen - der of the Faith was he, Called prea - cher, wri - ter,
3. Pro- claim - er of the i - con's role To tes - ti - fy the
4. A sing - er of the Tri - ni - ty Was John, whose hymns will
5. To You, O Fa - ther, source and end, To You, O Christ, both

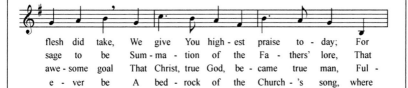

flesh did take, We give You high - est praise to - day; For
sage to be Sum - ma - tion of the Fa - thers' lore, That
awe - some goal That Christ, true God, be - came true man, Ful -
e - ver be A bed - rock of the Church - 's song, where
Lord and friend, To You, O Spi - rit, grace - 's spring, O

saint - ly John our thanks we pay.
we be faith - ful, as be - fore.
fill - ing thus His sa - ving plan.
truth and beau - ty fight the wrong.
Three - in - One, our praise we bring.

© 2013, J. Michael Thompson

SECTION V

MARTYRS OF THE

TWENTIETH CENTURY

ANDRIJ DEMIANCZUK

The Soviet KGB watched Charnetsky
constantly, and yet he was able to
prepare candidates for ordination
without being detected.

XIII

OUR BLESSED FATHER, MARTYR-BISHOP NICHOLAS CHARNETSKY

Feast Day: June 27

One of the synonyms for bishop is the word "pontiff," which comes from the Latin word *pontifex*—that is, a builder of bridges. The life of Blessed Nicholas Charnetsky (1884–1959) is an excellent example of this gift.

In a tiny village in the province of Galicia in what was then the Austro-Hungarian Empire, a child was born to Alexander and Parasceva Charnetsky on December 14, 1884. He was the first-born of what would eventually be a family of nine children. His parents named him Nicholas. Like most of their neighbors, they were members of the Ukrainian Greek Catholic Church. In most ways the Church is identical to the Orthodox Church, but it is in full communion with the pope.

Since his early youth, Nicholas told his parents he wanted to be a priest when he grew up, and this met with their approval. When he turned eighteen, the local bishop blessed him to study at the Ukrainian College in Rome. He completed his formation there and was eventually ordained a priest in 1909. His bishop then told him to begin working on his doctorate in sacred theology in Rome. Once he accomplished this, he was assigned the task of teaching in the eparchial seminary at Stanislaviv. Nicholas taught dogmatic theology and philosophy, having also been appointed as spiritual director to the students of the seminary. He carried out these tasks with great skill and was highly regarded by his fellow faculty and the students he taught.

After World War I, the huge Austro-Hungarian Empire was dismantled, and Galicia became part of the newly independent state of Poland. Religious life had been calling Charnetsky, enticing him to a more ascetic life. Providentially, the Congregation of the Most Holy Redeemer (the Redemptorists) established a mission in Galicia. Part of the mission included setting up a novitiate near the city of L'viv in 1919. With his bishop's permission, Nicholas entered the Redemptorist community. After he was received to first profession, the Redemptorists assigned him initially to parish work. His academic skills, however, influenced the community to appoint him as a professor at the Redemptorist seminary for high school boys, where he taught them with great success.

In 1926, Charnetsky was assigned to Volhynia, where the population had far more Eastern Orthodox than Greek Catholics. Because of Nicholas' desire to help improve relations between his fellow Greek Catholics and the members of the Orthodox Church, he came to be deeply appreciated by the people of both Churches. It was predominantly because of the success of this work that he was raised to the episcopacy of the Greek Catholic Church. Nicholas was consecrated as titular bishop of Lebed and appointed by Pope Pius XII as apostolic visitator for the Greek Catholics of both Volhynia and Pidlashia.

When World War II broke out, Poland was invaded from two directions. The Nazi army entered from the West and the Soviet army from the East. Eventually the Redemptorists were forced to leave Volhynia and moved to the city of L'viv.

In 1941, after two years of Soviet rule, the Ukrainian Greek Catholic Church reopened the L'viv Theological Academy and called Bishop

Nicholas to the faculty. Toward the end of World War II, the Soviet Army returned and seized all of the province of Galicia, incorporating it into the Ukrainian S.S.R. After having seized the territory, they proceeded to arrest every Greek Catholic bishop in order to facilitate the liquidation of the Greek Catholic Church. Property belonging to the Greek Catholic Church was seized and forcibly transferred to the Russian Orthodox Church. While in prison, Bishop Nicholas was beaten and subjected to lengthy "interviews" by the secret police. Eventually he was tried and convicted of "working with the German occupation forces" as well as for being a "secret agent for a non-Soviet power" (that is, the Vatican). He was exiled to a labor camp and almost worked to death.

The Soviet authorities decided to release Bishop Nicholas in 1956, because they expected him to die soon. God surprised them. While the bishop never completely regained his health, he became healthy enough to exercise some oversight over the Greek Catholic community that worshiped "in the catacombs," hidden from the civil authorities. One of his duties was to train young men for holy orders and to ordain them when he considered them spiritually ready. The KGB (Soviet Committee for State Security) watched him constantly, and yet he was able to prepare candidates for ordination without bring detected.

God called Bishop Nicholas to his eternal rest April 2, 1959. He was buried in the city of L'viv. In a very quiet way, people began making pilgrimages to his gravesite. Eventually, his religious community and the Vatican were notified of miraculous cures attributed to the bishop's intercession. Years later, the fact that he died as a confessor was confirmed. Along with Nicholas, many other confessors and martyrs of the Soviet era were beatified by Pope John Paul II in 2001. The date of the beatification has great meaning for the Redemptorist family, for it was celebrated June 27, the feast of the icon of Our Lady of Perpetual Help, the community's patronal feast.

SCRIPTURE

I charge you in the presence of God and of Christ Jesus, who will judge the living and the dead, and by his appearing and his kingly power:

proclaim the word; be persistent whether it is convenient or inconvenient; convince, reprimand, encourage through all patience and teaching.

For the time will come when people will not tolerate sound doctrine but, following their own desires and insatiable curiosity, will accumulate teachers

and will stop listening to the truth and will be diverted to myths.

But you, be self-possessed in all circumstances; put up with hardship; perform the work of an evangelist; fulfill your ministry.

For I am already being poured out like a libation, and the time of my departure is at hand.

I have competed well; I have finished the race; I have kept the faith.

From now on the crown of righteousness awaits me, which the Lord, the just judge, will award to me on that day, and not only to me, but to all who have longed for his appearance.

2 Timothy 4:1–8

QUOTATION

Blessed Nicholas, the prisoner and passion-bearer,
Calls us all to sing a hymn of deliverance:
"To the Redeemer and God who works wonders through me,
Let us sing!"

Troparion, Ode 1

REFLECTION

The life of a bishop is difficult, even in the best of times. In times of persecution, the bishop is called to lay down his life, if necessary, for the life of his sheep. How have I kept the bishops in my daily prayers, so they might be faithful to Christ Jesus and to his Church?

PRAYER

O Christ, you are the Redeemer who bought us back from sin and death when we had wandered far from you, and you loved us so much that you gave up your life on the cross for us. We thank you for the life and ministry of your holy bishop, Nicholas Charnetsky. He followed your call into the priesthood, and, to serve you even more deeply, he entered the Congregation of the Most Holy Redeemer, forming his life in the model of St. Alphonsus Liguori.

With great love, he worked for the salvation of souls in the Ukrainian Catholic Church, and in its defense he was imprisoned and tortured but never betrayed you or your Church. Give us, his sons and daughters, the same zeal for you and love for your Church, that we may grow in knowledge and love of you and come to be with you forever in heaven, where you, O Christ, live and reign with your Father and your Holy Spirit, now and ever and forever. Amen.

HYMN

Sing, O people! Join now
With the heavn'ly choir;
Raise your voice in gladness!
Pluck the harp and lyre!
Raise your voice in gladness!
Pluck the harp and lyre!

Nicholas the bishop
Pastored well his sheep
As did Christ, his Master—
Safe their souls did keep.
As did Christ, his Master—
Safe their souls did keep.

When the Church was threatened,
He gave up his life—
Bold, his faithful witness
In the face of strife.
Bold, his faithful witness
In the face of strife.

Praise to God the Father,
Son, and Spirit blest;
With our bishop martyr,
Bring Your flock to rest.
With our bishop martyr,
Bring Your flock to rest.

TUNE: *CHOLOVICHE DOBRYI / FAITHFUL CHRISTIANS*

TEXT: J. MICHAEL THOMPSON

A hymn for our Blessed Father Nicholas Charnetsky

tune: Choloviche Dobryi / Faithful Christians
author: V. Stekh (+1945)

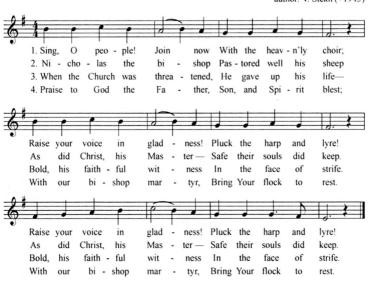

1. Sing, O peo - ple! Join now With the heav - n'ly choir;
2. Ni - cho - las the bi - shop Pas - tored well his sheep
3. When the Church was threa - tened, He gave up his life—
4. Praise to God the Fa - ther, Son, and Spi - rit blest;

Raise your voice in glad - ness! Pluck the harp and lyre!
As did Christ, his Mas - ter — Safe their souls did keep.
Bold, his faith - ful wit - ness In the face of strife.
With our bi - shop mar - tyr, Bring Your flock to rest.

Raise your voice in glad - ness! Pluck the harp and lyre!
As did Christ, his Mas - ter — Safe their souls did keep.
Bold, his faith - ful wit - ness In the face of strife.
With our bi - shop mar - tyr, Bring Your flock to rest.

© 2013, J. Michael Thompson

BLESSED THEODORE

HIEROMARTYR ROMZA

BISHOP of

MUKAČEVO

FR. ELIAS RAFAJ

Bishop Theodore Romzha protested against the Soviets' arrests of his priests and the confiscation of his churches, and, he said, "I would rather die than betray my Church."

XIV

OUR BLESSED
FATHER THEODORE ROMZHA,
MARTYR-BISHOP OF MUKACHEVO

Feast Day: October 31

What do Saints Thomas Becket, Thomas More, Josaphat of Polotsk, and Blessed Theodore Romzha of Mukachevo have in common? They were Christians who were put to death at least partially for their insistence that communion with the See of Peter was necessary for them and their local churches. This is underplayed in many of the current reflections on these martyrs, which makes it all the more important that we recognize it today.

Blessed Theodore was born in the Carpathian Mountains to Rusyn parents. Rusyns, also called "Ruthenians," are a Slavic people, but distinct from Russians, Ukrainians, and Slovaks. The greater part of the home territory of the Rusyns was once part of the Hungarian portion of the Austro-Hungarian Empire. After World War I, much of the territory became the eastern-most part of the newly created state of Czechoslovakia. Since World War II, Rusyn territory is divided between Ukraine and Slovakia, with parts of it in Hungary, Poland, and Romania as well.

Much of this description is necessary to understand the background of Theodore Romzha. He was born on April 14, 1911, in the village of Velykij

Bychkiv, in the province of Marmarosh, a Hungarian-ruled part of the Austro-Hungarian Empire. His father and mother, Pavel and Maria, were a middle-class couple who were members of the Greek Catholic Church. The family was bilingual and therefore capable of speaking both Rusyn (a Slavic tongue) and Hungarian, a not uncommon skill for the middle class of the time.

While his parents had hoped he would become a doctor or a lawyer, he told them he wanted to pursue the priesthood. Theodore did not have a high school in his town, so he had to travel to the gymnasium in the city of Chust. In Chust, he was a strong student and was highly regarded as an athlete. After he graduated, his bishop sent him to Rome, where he studied for two years at the German-Hungarian Seminary and then transferred to the Pontifical Russian College (called "Russicum"). The Russicum was staffed by the Jesuits and focused its attention on the study of liturgy as well as the conversion of Russia.

Theodore had heard the call of the Holy Father, who sought brave young men to go into the Soviet Union and do missionary work. Along with his seminary studies, he also learned the Russian language and studied about communism. This would all become very useful for him, though not in the way he imagined.

Theodore was made a priest on Christmas Day 1936 in the Basilica of Santa Maria Maggiore in Rome. He returned home to celebrate his first divine liturgy with the people of his native village, with the intention of returning to Rome to earn his doctorate. While in Czechoslovakia, he was drafted into the army to defend the country against the German invasion of the Sudetenland in the far western part of the land. He remained in the army until 1938.

Theodore's bishop decided to assign him to a small country parish in the village of Berezovo, where he was poor like the people he served. He remained there when the Hungarian army invaded Czechoslovakia and forcibly annexed the whole province into Hungary. This forced a restructuring of the Eparchy of Mukachevo, which sent Theodore to the city of Uzhhorod to become part of the faculty at the Greek Catholic Seminary there. He was assigned the posts of professor of philosophy and that of spiritual director. Blessed Theodore was known to be a strict teacher but a loving spiritual father to his seminarians. While residing in the seminary, he gave as generously as was possible to the poor of the city.

In the spring of 1943, the bishop of Mukachevo died. Rome intended to appoint the bishop of Hajdudorog (a Greek Catholic eparchy in Hungary) as the *locum tenens* of the Eparchy of Mukachevo. As the rapid approach of the Soviet army into the Sub-Carpathians became a reality, Rome chose to have Theodore Romzha consecrated as bishop and appointed him the apostolic administrator of the Eparchy of Mukachevo. His consecration took place September 24, 1944, and was soon followed by the invasion of the Soviet army. This eventually resulted in the annexation of the whole Sub-Carpathian region into the Ukrainian S.S.R.

New civil authorities began a systematic persecution of the Greek Catholic Church soon after the arrival of Soviet troops. When Bishop Theodore protested against the arrest of his priests and the confiscation of his churches, he was told in no uncertain terms that the persecution could stop immediately if Bishop Romzha would agree to forsake his eparchy's ties with Rome and fold his church into the Russian Orthodox Church. He said to the Soviet official who offered him this choice, "I would rather die than betray my Church." Theodore was speaking of the Greek Catholic Church in union with the pope in Rome.

Thus began an active campaign to cause priests and people to leave the Greek Catholic Church. This involved the arrests of priests and the closure or confiscation of Greek Catholic churches and institutions. Bishop Theodore traveled all over the eparchy in a horse-drawn wagon trying to keep his priests and people from losing heart. Returning home to Uzhhorod after one of those trips in 1947, his vehicle was struck by a Soviet military truck. Men came out of the truck and beat the bishop and his companions very badly. Fortunately, a civilian vehicle appeared and frightened the soldiers away. The civilians got the battered clergy into the city of Uzhhorod and to the hospital. Under the care of the nursing nuns at the hospital, the bishop's health began to improve. This recovery was halted on the night of October 31, when a new doctor and nurse took over that wing of the hospital. During that night, Bishop Romzha died. The Soviet authorities said in a press release that his death resulted from injuries connected with the auto accident, but it was learned that the nurse had poisoned him with a strong drug.

Bishop Theodore Romzha was buried from Holy Cross Cathedral in Uzhhorod, with thousands of his people in the streets of Uzhhorod for the funeral—this despite the efforts of the local government to keep them away. He was buried in the crypt of the cathedral. Two years later (1949), there was an announcement that the Greek Catholic Church had reunited itself with the Russian Orthodox Church. From that time until the Gorbachev Spring in 1988, the Church remained illegal, though active "in the catacombs."

After the Church came out of hiding, the relics of Bishop Theodore were disinterred and taken to Budapest to undergo medical examination. It was determined from DNA testing that these were, indeed, the bones of the martyred bishop. In 2001, during his visit to Ukraine, John Paul II beatified Theodore Romzha and acknowledged him as a martyr for the faith. On June 28, 2003, his relics were carried in procession through the streets of Uzhhorod and placed in a side chapel of Holy Cross Cathedral (which had been won back from the Russian Orthodox Diocese of Mukachevo). His feast day is October 31, the day of his death. The Eparchy of Mukachevo also keeps as a secondary feast June 28, which is the anniversary of the translation of his relics.

SCRIPTURE

Let what you heard from the beginning remain in you. If what you heard from the beginning remains in you, then you will remain in the Son and in the Father.

And this is the promise that he made us: eternal life.

I write you these things about those who would deceive you.

As for you, the anointing that you received from him remains in you, so that you do not need anyone to teach you. But his anointing teaches you about everything and is true and not false; just as it taught you, remain in him.

1 John 2:24–27

QUOTATION

Though the godless poured poison into your veins,

your heart still beats with love for Christ,

O bishop Theodore, martyred father,

who now raise your prayers before the throne of God.

KONTAKION, TONE 8

REFLECTION

Blessed Theodore was a gifted man intellectually who never feared to work with the poor and unlearned people in a parish. He loved the poor and cared for them assiduously. When the Communists came to power, they offered him both wealth and authority if he would only publicly betray the Greek Catholic Church. He refused, and for this refusal he was killed. In our daily life, we often have small opportunities either to profess our faith or to hide it. How are we showing forth our commitment to Jesus Christ?

PRAYER

O Christ, the Good Shepherd of your Church, we give you thanks for the life and witness of your bishop, Theodore Romzha. Early in life, he heard the call to follow and serve you as a priest. Leaving home and family, he went to seminary in his own land and then in far-off Rome. In his studies, he sought to deepen his knowledge and love of you and of your holy Church. Returning to his land and people, he served the poorest of the poor with care and devotion and became greatly loved by those who were in his charge.

Called from the work of a parish pastor, he taught and guided the young men of the eparchy as they, too, studied for the priesthood. In a time of extreme strife and danger, he was called to be bishop of the Church of Mukachevo. Loyal both to his local Church and to the See of Rome, he shepherded his flock and defended them, even so far as giving his life for them. We ask that you bless us with the same determination to remain faithful to you and your Church, O Christ, and to spread the Good News into every corner of the world. For you, O Christ our God, gave up your life willingly for your sheep. We give you glory along with your Father without beginning and your all-holy, good, and life-giving Spirit, now and ever and forever. Amen.

HYMN

Christians, come with hymns of gladness;
For this day, with joy o'erflowing,
Bids us set aside all sadness:
God His peace is here bestowing.

Theodore, our faithful shepherd,
On this day was crowned with glory;
Having suffered for his Master,
Now his people tell his story.

Theodore was ever faithful
In the face of all temptation
To his Church and to his people,
Through the fiercest tribulation.

Give us grace, his zeal to copy;
As he strove the faith to nourish,
So inspire us by his actions
That we each your Church will cherish.

In communion with our martyr,
We this song of praise now render
To you, Father, Son, and Spirit,
Triune God, in heaven's splendor.

TUNE: *CHRISTIJANE, PRIBIHAJTE* / *CHRISTIANS, JOIN IN OUR PROCESSION*

TEXT: J. MICHAEL THOMPSON

A hymn for our Blessed Father Theodore Romzha

tune: Christijane, pribihajte / Christians, Join in Our Procession
source: Carpatho-Rusyn melody

1. Chris - tians,   come   with   hymns   of   glad - ness;
2. The - o - dore,   our   faith - ful   shep - herd,
3. The - o - dore   was   ev - er   faith - ful
4. Give   us   grace,   his   zeal   to   cop - y;
5. In   com - mun - ion   with   our   mar - tyr,

For   this   day,   with   joy   o'er - flow - ing,
On   this   day   was   crowned   with   glo - ry;
In   the   face   of   all   temp - ta - tion
As   he   strove   the   faith   to   nour - ish,
We   this   song   of   praise   now   ren - der

Bids   us   set   a - side   all   sad - ness:
Hav - ing   suf - fered   for   his   Mas - ter,
To   his   Church   and   to   his   peo - ple,
So   in - spire   us   by   his   ac - tions
To   you,   Fa - ther,   Son,   and   Spir - it,

God   His   peace   is   here   be - stow - ing.
Now   his   peo - ple   tell   his   sto - ry.
Through   the   fier - cest   tri - bu - la - tion.
That   we   each   your   Church   will   cher - ish.
Tri - une   God,   in   heav - en's   splen - dor.

© 2002, J. Michael Thompson

BL METOD DOMINIK

Віфлеємі
Новна
Діва
Сина
зроднла

MIRON KERUL-KMEC, JR.

In 1950, Redemptorists were imprisoned in detention camps and underwent intense questioning, brainwashing, and torture. Trcka tried to shield his brothers and calmly endured torture.

XV

OUR BLESSED VENERABLE
CONFESSOR
METHODIUS DOMINIC TRCKA

Feast Day: August 25

The twentieth century was a time of many changes. One of these was the development of biritual clergy. That is, men ordained into the Roman rite who were given permission from both their Roman-rite bishop and from a bishop of one of the Eastern Catholic Churches to celebrate the holy mysteries in the tradition of that specific Eastern church. This last person in our book was not only given these biritual faculties, but he requested and was given a canonical transfer from the Latin Church to the Greek Catholic Church.

Dominic Trcka was born on July 6, 1886, in the Bohemian province of the Austro-Hungarian Empire. He was of Czech descent and grew up in a Roman Catholic family. When he was sixteen, he was received into the novitiate of the Redemptorist congregation. Two years later, he made his life profession in the congregation, and was sent to study theology. On July 17, 1910, Dominic was ordained to the holy priesthood, and the Redemptorists assigned him the work of being a mission preacher.

During World War I, Central Europe was overrun with displaced persons. During this time, Trcka worked with refugees from Croatia,

Slovenia, and with Rusyns. After the war, he requested permission from his superiors to work full time with the Greek Catholics in Czechoslovakia (newly created in 1918). The congregation sent him to work with the Greek Catholics in the city of L'viv. He was greatly aided in this new work by his confrere, Bishop Nicholas Charnetsky, who also helped him to learn the language of the people for whom he was caring. It was at this time that, with the permission of his superiors, he took the new name of "Methodius," making a radical identification of himself with the "Apostle of the Slavs" who had given his life to evangelizing the Slavic people in their own language.

Trcka was posted in 1921 to the city of Stropkov in the eastern part of the province of Slovakia. It was there that he founded the first mixed Latin and Byzantine rite Redemptorist monastery, which consisted of both Roman Catholic and Greek Catholic priests and brothers. Trcka was the first superior of that community. From there, he was a fervent preacher among the Greek Catholic Eparchies of Mukachevo and Preshov in Czechoslovakia, and Krizhevci in Yugoslavia. During his first term as superior, he supervised the first Greek Catholic Redemptorist monastery in the city of Kosice.

Methodius' heavy workload caused him to fall ill, and in 1932 his superiors decided to have him return to Stropkov, where he was supposed to rest. While there, he undertook parish work in the town. By 1935, he was reassigned to Michalovce. It was from there that he accepted a new assignment from the Congregation for the Oriental Churches. He was commissioned as the apostolic visitator to the sisters of the Order of St. Basil the Great, a Greek Catholic women's community with monasteries in the Eparchies of Preshov and Mukachevo.

His second term as superior of the Redemptorist monastery in Michalovce (1935–1942) included such major events as the construction of the monastery church, the erection of a convent, and two retreat centers (one in Michalovce and one in Uzhhorod, in the Eparchy of Mukachevo).

The Second World War brought many changes to Czechoslovakia. The Germans invaded and annexed the Sudetenland from the province of Bohemia. The country itself was split into two separate countries. Slovakia became an independent fascist state, with most of the Eparchy of Mukachevo seized by Hungary. The Greek Catholics of the Eparchy of Presov were left in the new Slovak state, which resented the presence of non-Slovaks in the country. At this time, the Slovak government placed the Redemptorists under special scrutiny, since their mission was to the Greek Catholics (called Ruthenians by the government). This made Trcka a prime suspect. He took much of that burden upon his own shoulders to divert attention away from the other Redemptorists.

At the end of World War II, the Redemptorist community established a Redemptorist Greek Catholic vice province, and on March 23, 1946, Trcka was asked to be the first vice provincial. It was he who encouraged the return of the Redemptorists to their former house in Stropkov. All of this was brought to a brutal end as the Communist Party came to power in Czechoslovakia in 1948. One of their first official acts was the suppression of the vice province. In the spring of 1950, the Redemptorists of the vice province were imprisoned in detention camps, where they underwent intense questioning, brainwashing, and torture. His Redemptorist brethren told of Trcka's constant attempt to shield his brothers and of his calm endurance of brutal treatment.

Trcka was officially accused of collaboration with the Greek Catholic bishop of Preshov, Kyr Pavel Gojdich. This, of course, was viewed as treasonous by the new government because Bishop Gojdich was a Rusyn. Trcka was seen to be stirring up Rusyn nationalism in Slovakia by sharing the bishop's pastoral letters. Since he had also continued sending regular reports to his superiors in the Redemptorist community in Prague, and, through them, to the Vatican, he was accused of espionage and high treason.

In April 1952, Trcka was sentenced to a prison camp for a period of twelve years. Though he was already in poor health, he refused to give in to the efforts of his Communist jailers to break him. In 1958, he was transferred to the prison at Leopoldov. On Christmas of that year, he was overheard singing a Rusyn Christmas carol in his prison cell. This resulted in him being moved to a correction cell, where Trcka developed pneumonia. When a fellow prisoner, a medical doctor, requested that the priest be allowed to go to the infirmary, the guards took him instead to a cell of solitary confinement, where he died on March 23, 1959. With his last words, he forgave those who persecuted him. He was buried in the prison cemetery in Leopoldov. In 1969, his remains were transferred from there to the Redemptorist church at Michalovce.

Methodius Dominic Trcka was declared a martyr for the faith, and Pope John Paul II beatified him with others on November 4, 2001.

SCRIPTURE

The end of all things is at hand. Therefore, be serious and sober for prayers.

Above all, let your love for one another be intense, because love covers a multitude of sins.

Be hospitable to one another without complaining.

As each one has received a gift, use it to serve one another as good stewards of God's varied grace.

Whoever preaches, let it be with the words of God; whoever serves, let it be with the strength that God supplies, so that in all things God may be glorified through Jesus Christ, to whom belong glory and dominion forever and ever. Amen.

1 PETER 4:7–11

QUOTATION

Glory of the ranks of the Redemptorists,

honor of the Carpathian mountains,

O blessed confessor and priest-martyr Dominic Methodius,

you were faithful to the Gospel of redeeming love

from your first vows until your final breath,

building up the Church which adopted you

serving by preaching and teaching.

Now we sing your praise and glorify your sufferings:

Rejoice, O father, confessor and martyr!

KONTAKION, TONE 4

REFLECTION

Blessed Methodius gave up everything familiar to him so that he could minister faithfully to the Greek Catholic faithful in Central Europe. In doing so, he echoed the words of St. Paul, "becoming all things to all men so as to save some." Many people consider him to be the unofficial patron saint of those who grew up in a one-ritual church and then received permission to change to another, the better to follow God's will. Even if this is not what God is asking of us, there is no question that the will of God often takes us to new places and has us interact with new people. When God calls us to new experiences, are we open to hear his voice?

PRAYER

O merciful Lord Jesus Christ, you have given your Church an example of priestly zeal and courage in our Blessed and Venerable Father Methodius Dominic Trcka. Urged on by love of you, his Redeemer, he sought out the brotherhood of Alphonsus Liguori, who formed him and nurtured him. In response to your call, he came to minister to the displaced members of the Greek Catholic Church, and, with the permission of his superiors, cast his lot with them. Changing his very name, he became a model for Eastern Catholic priests in his zeal for the traditions of the East. Faithful to you, he endured imprisonment and torture and even solitary death for the glory of your name. Teach us to emulate his love for you, our Redeemer and Lord, and for the Church that embodies your message of grace and truth. We glorify you with your Father without beginning and your good and life-creating Spirit, now and always and forever and ever. Amen.

HYMN

Lord, in Your mercy, You give ev'ry nation
Priests in Your image, preaching Your salvation.
Now on this day, we raise hymns of glory—
Blessed Methodius is our theme, our story!

Come to our aid in times of war and sadness,
Learning our ways and teaching Christ in gladness
He guided well his brethren in striving,
Modeling Jesus in his life and dying.

When taken off to prison cruel and ruthless,
He persevered in song and pray'r so ceaseless
That guards, despising these hymns so holy,
Left him to die in solitude most lowly.

Glory to God, Father, Son, and Holy Spirit,
Who wills His saints heaven to inherit.
With good Methodius, leading us in singing,
Let us daily strive, Your Kingdom to be bringing!

TUNE: *VO VYFLEJEMI* / *IN BETHLEHEM*

TEXT: J. MICHAEL THOMPSON

A hymn for our Blessed Venerable Confessor Methodius Dominic Trcka

tune: Vo Vyflejemi / In Bethlehem
author: O. Nyzhankovs'kyi (1919)

1. Lord, in Your mer - cy, You give ev' - ry na - tion
2. Come to our aid in times of war and sad - ness,
3. When ta - ken off to pri - son cruel and ruth - less,
4. Glo - ry to God, Fa - ther, Son, and Ho - ly Spi - rit,

Priests in Your im - age, preach-ing Your sal - va - tion.
Learn - ing our ways and teach - ing Christ in glad - ness
He per - se - vered in song and pray'r so cease - less
Who wills His saints hea - ven to in - her - it.

Now on this day, we raise hymns of glo - ry—
He guid - ed well his breth - ren in stri - ving,
That guards, de - spi - sing these hymns so ho - ly,
With good Me - tho - dius, lead-ing us in sing - ing,

Bles - sed Me - tho - dius is our theme, our sto - ry!
Mo - del - ing Je - sus in his life and dy - ing.
Left him to die in so - li - tude most low - ly.
Let us dai - ly strive, Your King - dom to be bring-ing!

© 2013, J. Michael Thompson

SOURCES OF "QUOTATIONS"

Introduction: Troparion from Ode 6, Canon of All Saints' Sunday, page 4, *Pentecostarion*, Sisters of the Order of St. Basil the Great, Uniontown, Pennsylvania, 1986.

I: Troparion, Tone 2, page 44, *Byzantine Monthly Menaion*, Volume Four: December. Metropolitan Cantor Institute, Pittsburgh, 2005.

II: Troparion, Tone 4, translated from the Byzantine text by J. Michael Thompson.

III: Kontakion, Tone 4, page 7, *Byzantine Monthly Menaion*, Volume Four: December. Metropolitan Cantor Institute, Pittsburgh, 2005.

IV: Kontakion, Tone 4, page 54, *Byzantine Monthly Menaion*, Volume Eleven: July. Metropolitan Cantor Institute, Pittsburgh, 2005.

V: Kontakion, Tone 8, page 10, *Byzantine Monthly Menaion*, Volume Four: December. Metropolitan Cantor Institute, Pittsburgh, 2005.

VI: Kontakion, Tone 4, page 80, *Byzantine Monthly Menaion*, Volume Five: January. Metropolitan Cantor Institute, Pittsburgh, 2005.

VII: Kontakion, Tone 3, page 29, *Byzantine Monthly Menaion*, Volume Six: May. Metropolitan Cantor Institute, Pittsburgh, 2005.

VIII: Troparion, Tone 8, page 7, *Byzantine Monthly Menaion*, Volume Nine: May. Metropolitan Cantor Institute, Pittsburgh, 2005.

IX: Kontakion, Tone 2, page 68, *Byzantine Monthly Menaion*, Volume Ten: June. Metropolitan Cantor Institute, Pittsburgh, 2005.

X: Kontakion, Tone 8, page 69, *Byzantine Monthly Menaion*, Volume Five: January. Metropolitan Cantor Institute, Pittsburgh, 2005.

XI: Troparion, Tone 8, page 36, *Byzantine Monthly Menaion*, Volume Three: November. Metropolitan Cantor Institute, Pittsburgh, 2005.

XII: Kontakion, Tone 4, page 8, *Byzantine Monthly Menaion*, Volume Four: December. Metropolitan Cantor Institute, Pittsburgh, 2005.

XIII: Troparion, Ode 1, *Canon to the New Martyrs*; translation from Ukrainian to English for this book by Fr. Peter Galadza, PhD.

XIV: Kontakion, Tone 8, page 1, *Byzantine Monthly Menaion*, Volume Three: November. Metropolitan Cantor Institute, Pittsburgh, 2005.

XV: Kontakion, Tone 4, composed by J. Michael Thompson.

CPSIA information can be obtained at www.ICGtesting.com
Printed in the USA
LVOW10s0413211013

357691LV00005B/11/P

9 780764 823374